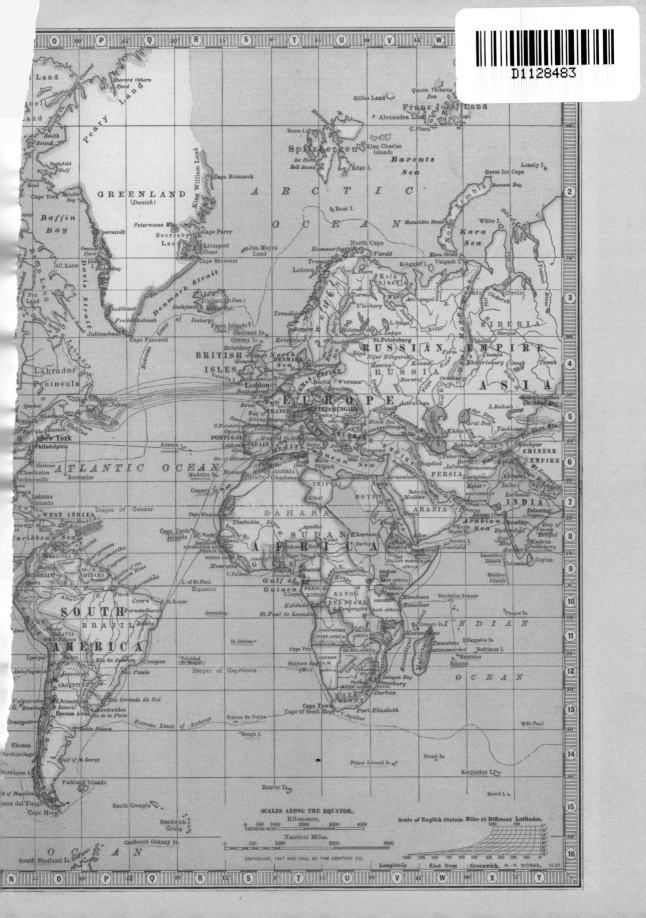

THE
VICTORIANS

FROM EMPIRE AND INDUSTRY
TO POVERTY AND FAMINE

THE
VICTORIANS

FROM EMPIRE AND INDUSTRY
TO POVERTY AND FAMINE

JOHN D. WRIGHT

amber
BOOKS

Published by Amber Books Ltd
United House
London N7 9DP
United Kingdom
www.amberbooks.co.uk
Appstore: itunes.com/apps/amberbooksltd
Facebook: www.facebook.com/amberbooks
Twitter: @amberbooks

ISBN: 978-1-78274-588-4

Project Editor: Michael Spilling
Designer: Zoë Mellors
Picture Researcher: Terry Forshaw

Printed in China

Contents

1

THE CITY

Mention of the Victorians will naturally call up thoughts of London. Vivid images of the city were captured by writers such as Charles Dickens and Arthur Conan Doyle, while newspapers added real criminal horror, covering Jack the Ripper and other murderers.

L ONDON WAS the home of comfortable Victorian families who supported morality and the best of British traditions. Those in the fine houses of the rising middle class, however, were acutely aware of the poverty, disease and crime festering in the background. This was often brought into their own houses by the unfortunate servants who laboured downstairs. Both rich and poor seemed resigned to inequality and to the immense human problems caused by the city's rapid growth.

Victorian 'progress' was the surprising cause of these dreadful conditions. The Industrial Revolution, which had begun in Britain in about 1760, was in full force by the mid-nineteenth century as factories relied on more and larger machines for mass production. This job-destroying efficiency had already provoked the Luddites, redundant textile workers in Nottinghamshire,

Opposite: This 'Bandits' Roost' in a New York slum was photographed by Jacob Riis in 1888.

Yorkshire and Lancashire, who wrecked machinery between 1811 and 1813 and in later sporadic attacks, including in southern England. Many early leaders were tried and hanged or transported to the colonies.

Industries including textiles and ceramics lured workers from the fields to the cities. By 1851, Britain's urban population was larger than its rural one. The rush from the land created overcrowded and filthy cities, where many ambitions died in slums and workhouses. The large numbers of skilled and unskilled workers kept wages down to barely subsistence level. The result was an increase in violent crime, robbery, prostitution, alcoholism and early death, often from unhealthy food and sickness.

While London was the emblem of the Victorian age – after all, the queen reigned among its residents – these effects were equally felt in Britain's industrial powerhouses, such as Birmingham and Manchester, as well as in the growing world cities. Although Victorians were eager for progress, they faced uncertainties in their daily lives, resulting in frustration and anxiety that often

Below: An agitator of the destructive Luddites was depicted wearing women's clothes in this political satire.

Drawn from Life by an Officer

THE LEADER of the LUDDITES

Publ. May 1812 by Messrs. Walker and Knight, Sweetings Alley, Royal Exchange.

led to violence. This was not confined to Britain, as seen in the 1863 Draft Riots in New York City and the Paris Commune insurrection in 1871.

Above: The 'dark satanic mills' of the industrial revolution condemned workers to a life of misery and hopelessness.

POVERTY

Victorians believed that the poor had caused their own situation, either through laziness and refusal to work or because they drank, gambled or wasted money. To some, there appeared to be a natural order in which superior people led decent, secure lives and inferior types were condemned to terrible poverty. A survey in 1886 found that one-third of London's residents were poor. Some paid one penny to sleep in shelters provided in the city. One run by the Salvation Army in Blackfriars in the 1890s offered its only sleeping places in wooden boxes called 'coffin beds', on benches, or on the floor.

Poverty was also thought to be a crime that was morally wrong and one that should be punished with prison. Charles Dickens provided the best-known descriptions of London's

Above: A cartoon
published in *Punch*
magazine in 1858 depicted
death amid the sewage
and pollution in the
River Thames.

debtors' prisons.
His father John
and his family had
been sentenced to
Marshalsea Prison in
Southwark in 1824
over a £40 debt to a
baker. Charles, then 12,
had to quit school and
work polishing shoes
in a blacking factory
to help his family. He
wrote about these
experiences in *Little
Dorrit*, serialized from
1855 to 1857.

Dickens' case was not unusual for Victorians: about 10,000
debtors were imprisoned each year. This could mean an
indefinite stay until the money was repaid – not an easy task
because prisoners were forced to pay for their rooms and meals.
The Debtors' Act was passed by Parliament in 1869 to stop
imprisonment, but those who owed money could still be locked
up if they had the necessary funds but refused to pay. By 1900,
the prisons still contained 11,427 debtors.

One step above prison was the workhouse, where paupers
could live under harsh controls and work to improve their moral
character. The sick and elderly were also taken in, while many
others were orphans, widows with young children, wives who
had been deserted, and 'fallen women'. The conditions were
purposely unpleasant to discourage people from applying or
extending their stay.

DIRTY LONDON

Life in the city was filthy. Streets were caked with mud and the
droppings of horses and other animals, while the hazy air was
choked with fog, smoke and soot. Cesspools in the basements of
houses often became blocked and overran, adding to the general

stench. When water closets became popular, the raw sewage was run into pipes built to transport rainwater into the Thames. This was to be cleaned as drinking water, but resulted in diseases such as cholera and typhoid. The river's dreadful smell increased until the 'Great Stink' of 1858 occurred. Members of Parliament suffered so much that the curtains of the House of Commons were soaked in chloride of lime to try to block the stench. The effort proved unsuccessful, so the members passed a law to construct a new sewer system.

The Victorian age's polluted cities greatly shortened a person's lifespan, especially for the poor who were crowded into slums. In 1851, someone living in the small market town of Okehampton had a life expectancy of 57 years, compared to 26 for a resident of inner Liverpool. Home coal fires and factory fumes caused respiratory diseases and early deaths. Birmingham and Sheffield were more dangerous than London due to their intense coal burning for metal production.

LIFE IN A DEBTORS' PRISON

INMATES IN DEBTORS' prisons lived, strangely enough, in a type of community organization run by their own committees. Families could live there with the debtor, and children were born and raised in the prison. Debtors with more money than others were allowed better quarters closer to the prison master. They were allowed visitors who might provide funds so the inmates could pay for items at the prison shop and restaurant, and even spend time outside. The poorest, however, made do with the barest necessities in another wing, sharing rooms with others.

Right: If inmates had little money, they would find debtors' prison to be an overcrowded miserable existence.

THE TOOLEY STREET FIRE

Fire was a constant fear in Victorian cities, which were crowded with wooden buildings protected by inadequate fire brigades. Londoners were especially wary of the danger, mindful of the Great Fire of 1666 and the more recent memory of the Houses of Parliament burning down in 1834, three years before Victoria ascended the throne.

Another massive fire ravaged the city in 1861 and proved to be the largest since the Great Fire. It began on 22 June, a Saturday, at Cotton's Wharf on Tooley Street, among warehouses stacked with combustible goods, including hemp, jute, cotton, oil, paint, tallow and saltpetre. Spontaneous combustion of hemp was thought to be the cause, while carelessness increased the blaze, the iron fire doors having been left open.

By evening, the inferno stretched from London Bridge to Custom House. Even the surface of the Thames was burning from materials that had spilled onto it, destroying several boats. Fourteen fire engines tried to fight the flames with a low amount of water; even a floating fire engine failed because of the low tide. More tragedy occurred when the fire superintendent, James Braidwood, was killed as a warehouse collapsed on

Right: The ferocious Tooley Street fire shocked Londoners into providing a city-wide fire brigade to prevent future tragedies.

inn." It made one very sad", wrote Queen Victoria in her diary when told of his death. More than 30,000 Londoners gathered to watch the fire, enjoying refreshments sold by vendors and pubs that remained open throughout the night. The fire burned for two weeks and destroyed an estimated £2 million in goods and buildings.

The Tooley Street Fire led to an upgrading of London's fire services. The small London Fire Engine Establishment (LFEE), run by 25 insurance companies, was replaced in 1866 by a public service, the Metropolitan Fire Brigade.

INCREASED MIGRATION

The overcrowding of cities and harsh economics led to unprecedented emigration, both to and from Britain. Many left for America, Australia and various colonies. The Irish formed the largest number, with an estimated two million escaping the potato famine of 1845–49 to seek a better life in the United States and also in England and Scotland. The UK's growing industries also attracted migrants from Europe and more distant countries. One could walk London's streets and soon encounter

OTHER GREAT FIRES

WOODEN BUILDINGS IN CITIES around the world in Victorian times were crowded on narrow streets and packed with people who had to fend for themselves during major fires that exceeded the skills and resources of early firemen.

Hamburg lost a third of the buildings in its old district in 1842 when a fire began in a cigar factory and burned from 5 to 8 May. It killed 51 people and destroyed 1700 homes. The fire was the first to shake the new international insurance business, with many British insurers taking enormous losses. Bucharest was devastated on 23 March 1847 by a fire that levelled one-third of the city and virtually all of the central business area. It was started by a teenage boy firing a gun into a loft

Japanese, Chinese, Indian and Arab people. Many Jews settled in the city's East End, especially Spitalfields, and kept up their own language and traditions. They attracted sympathy at first after escaping the Russian pogroms and other persecutions, but the public attitude eventually turned against them. One leader of the anti-immigration movement, Arnold White, called the Jews 'a danger menacing to national life', and some members of Parliament unsuccessfully called for restrictions on general immigration.

of dry hay. Fifteen people were killed and 1850 buildings burned down, including 12 churches.

Chicago's great fire of 1871 burned from 8 to 10 October and destroyed roughly one-third of the city. It left 300 dead, 90,000 homeless and destroyed 17,450 buildings, resulting in $200 million in damage. Tradition says the blaze was caused by Mrs Catherine O'Leary's cow kicking over a lamp in a barn.

Hong Kong in 1878 suffered a great fire on Christmas night that destroyed several hectares of the city. Local photographers were selling pictures of the tragedy while the embers still smouldered. An English businessman, Edward Fisher, was accused of arson for insurance but was acquitted.

Left: The fire's terrible destruction of wooden buildings led to Chicago building the world's first steel skyscrapers.

Above: The potato famine of the 1840s drove millions of Irish to the United States to settle into equally desperate lives.

The most unpleasant migration out of Britain was enforced transportation. Those who broke the law – even for minor street crimes – might be shipped to overseas colonies for seven to 14 years, but often for the remainder of their lives. Even criminals due to be executed sometimes had their sentences reduced to transportation. The policy had begun in 1717, when convicts were sent to penal colonies in America. After that country's independence, Australia became the main destination. The system was flawed, adding political prisoners such as Irish nationalists and increasing shipments to provide Australia with needed cheap labour. Victorians began to regret this and the idea of giving criminals a free voyage to a new, if rugged, life. The practice was abolished in 1868, after the transport of 158,702 convicts in around 80 years.

IRISH SLUMS IN NEW YORK

The Irish who fled poverty in the Victorian era did not find the 'American Dream' in New York City. They were packed into dismal tenements in the city's Lower East Side, with nearly

TAMMANY HALL

THOMAS JEFFERSON, author of American's Declaration of Independence, observed his nation's growing population and worried about people 'piled high up on one another in the cities'. His prediction proved accurate by 1880, when the population of more than 50 million had created major cities. What he did not forecast was the enormous growth of city governments and corruption. Big-city political organizations could handle problems efficiently, but many members were keen to reward themselves and swap favours for patronage.

New York had one of the worst political machines in the Democratic Party's executive committee, known as Tammany Hall. Under its notorious William 'Boss' Tweed, it corrupted local elections, bribed rival politicians, and even influenced state and national politics. Its members had no qualms about a little honest graft. One, George Washington Plunkitt, made large profits from tips about land selected for parks and other major projects. He snapped up the properties and sold them to the city for inflated prices.

Tammany Hall outlived the Victorian era, but erred in not supporting Democratic candidate Franklin D. Roosevelt in his successful 1932 presidential race. He reduced the machine's power, aided by the new reformist mayor, Fiorello La Guardia.

Right: American artist Thomas Nash depicted the Tweed ring where each member points blame at the next person.

WHO STOLE THE PEOPLE'S MONEY? — DO TELL . N.Y. TIMES.   'TWAS HIM.

Above: New York's Draft Riots were a working class protest against conscription to fight in the Civil War.

300,000 occupying one square mile. One in four residents of Victorian New York was Irish. Sometimes five families would share one room in an apartment that had no toilet, bath or running water. This huddling together of humanity led rapidly to physical and moral decline, evident in epidemics and widespread drunkenness, crime and violence. Many Irish took part in the city's 1863 Draft Riots, in which more than 100 African Americans were killed.

Outside was no better. As in London and other overcrowded industrial Victorian cities, New York's streets were filled with animal and human waste, which promoted stench, disease and death. Children played in the filth next to dead horses and roaming pigs and drank contaminated milk sold by street vendors. About 25 per cent of the immigrant Irish children died.

Charles Dickens toured the Five Points area of Manhattan in 1842 accompanied by two policemen, because this was an Irish slum of utter poverty and degradation. In his *American Notes for General Circulation* published that year, he noted that 'poverty, wretchedness and vice are rife'. He described the area's narrow ways as 'reeking everywhere with dirt and filth'. However, he was quick to compare these conditions with those of other Victorian cities. 'Such lives as are led here,' he wrote, 'bear the same fruits here as elsewhere. The coarse and bloated faces at the doors have counterparts at home and all the wide world over'.

THE GANGS OF NEW YORK

The shocking violence on the streets of nineteenth-century New York was described in Herbert Asbury's 1927 book *The Gangs of New York*, filmed by Martin Scorsese in 2002. The basis for both was the underworld that existed in Manhattan's districts of Five Points, Hell's Kitchen and the Bowery, the homes of murderers, prostitutes, pickpockets and other thieves. The streets were ruled by such gangs as the Plug Uglies, the Forty Thieves, the Bowery Boys, the Daybreak Boys, the Whyos, and the Dead Rabbits. Their dangerous criminals bore frightening names such as Bill the Butcher, Ludwig the Bloodsucker, Hell-Cat Maggie, Eat 'Em Up Jack McManus, Slobbery Jim, Cow-legged Sam McCarthy, Sadie the Goat (who head-butted victims) and Dandy Johnny Dolan. The latter wore axe blades on his shoes and carried a copper eye gouger.

These gangs were so powerful and dangerous, they would post warnings for the police to stay out of their patches or pay the consequences. They also operated as political clubs supporting various candidates and owned legitimate businesses such as casinos and saloons. Sometimes gang members were business-like in a different way. Piker Ryan, a member of the Whyos, was once caught with a price list for his services, including a punch in the face for $2, crewing an ear off for $15 and murder, listed as 'doing the big job', for $100.

Below: The vicious Short Tail Gang in 1887 terrorized New York's Lower East Side and the docks.

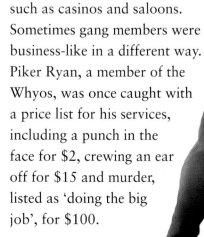

HELL-CAT MAGGIE

ONE OF THE MOST feared gang members in the Five Points district, Hell-Cat Maggie was an Irish immigrant first recruited by the Whyos as a thief. Graduating to violence, she joined the Dead Rabbits, filing her teeth to points and wearing razor-sharp brass fingernails into battle, often against the Bowery Boys.

She screamed as she charged enemies, clawing and biting. She particularly enjoyed tearing ears off victims and pickling them in alcohol for display behind the bar where she worked as a bouncer. Political parties also hired Maggie as a 'shoulder-hitter' to threaten or attack opponents during elections.

VIENNESE POVERTY

All the glories of music, architecture, culture and polite society could not hide Vienna's abject poverty in the Victorian years, when the city was ringed by slums and factories. Even Adolf Hitler fumed about the city's 'dazzling riches and loathsome poverty'. Vienna was overwhelmed by poor workers flooding in from the large Austrian Empire after the failed 1848 revolution. These newcomers were housed in the inner city in dreadful tenements with minimal sanitation. The poor seldom received medical treatment, and diseases, especially tuberculosis, cost many lives. Among its victims were the homeless, some of whom lived in the city sewers. Hungry people, many of them children, scraped through rubbish in the streets in search of kitchen waste. By 1891, only one-third of the population had been born in the city. The population of 1.5 million ranked only after London and Paris, but in 1894 Vienna exceeded those cities in its degree of poverty.

THE POPULATION OF 1.5 MILLION RANKED ONLY AFTER LONDON AND PARIS, BUT IN 1894 VIENNA EXCEEDED THOSE CITIES IN ITS DEGREE OF POVERTY.

CHILD LABOUR

Dickens became the best-known victim of the Victorians' use of working children who had their education cut short and their

health often seriously endangered. Yet his work polishing shoes was mild compared to the rough labour of many boys and girls who worked as chimney sweeps, coal miners and workers in factories, shipyards and farms. At the age of five, boys were working in coal mines and girls in domestic service. In many instances, they were badly treated and physically abused. When laws were passed, they only limited the hours and ages of child workers. The Factory and Workshop Act of 1878 banned work for children younger than 10. By 1891, more than 100,000 girls aged 10 to 14 were still in domestic service.

Child welfare did slowly improve; by the end of Victoria's reign, most children were schooled to the age of 12. While one-third of boys and girls had received no education in 1852, this had increased to nearly 90 per cent in 1899 for children up to eight years old.

CHILD ABUSE

Two notions intended to better the Victorian family often led to difficult childhoods. The father was considered to be in charge of his family, and he often dealt out strict discipline. This could be administered by a nanny if one was employed, and some proved to be intolerant and mean. Punishments such as moderate smacking and even blows using belts or other instruments were deemed to be family matters. The same painful treatment of

Above: An 1866 engraving depicts child labourers struggling to move coal from the coalface in an English mine.

CHARLES DICKENS

BORN IN 1812, Charles Dickens quickly came face to face with Victorian society's unjust economic and social conditions. Besides being the most popular novelist of that era, Dickens used his stories to expose London's poverty and social wrongs.

Above: Dickens had to leave school and do manual work in a factory but became the world's most popular Victorian author.

Some scenes came from his family's life, as when Mr Micawber was imprisoned for debt in *David Copperfield* (1850). He levelled criticism at such sensitive topics as education, public opinion, greed, selfishness and the lack of sympathy for the poor and vulnerable. His despair was expressed in novels such as *Oliver Twist* (1838) and *Bleak House* (1853) and increased in his last finished work, *Our Mutual Friend* (1865).

Dickens also despaired about industrial pollution, as seen in *Hard Times* (1854), where a mill town's tall chimneys were 'puffing out their poisonous volumes' until domestic windows 'showed the Coketown people a sun eternally in eclipse, through a medium of smoked glass'.

Along with his fame, Dickens was also a philanthropist, working to right the many social problems he wrote about. He helped establish a safe house in Shepherd's Bush to aid destitute girls and women who had fallen into prostitution and crime. Another project supported Ragged Schools for poor children, since he believed that education was the best cure for crime and poverty.

young servants and pupils drew little concern, giving sadistic employees and teachers a free hand.

Children from poor families suffered more. They usually had tiring jobs from a young age and might return home to alcoholic, violent parents who abused them. Many boys and girls chose to live mostly on the streets, often as runaways, and some fell prey to thieving or prostitution to obtain food and shelter. In 1848, nearly 2700 girls aged 11 to 16 were admitted to London hospitals for venereal diseases, most resulting from prostitution. The sexual exploitation of children, including rape and incest, was widespread and the Victorian public somewhat hypocritical in condemning without acting. Churches and charity organizations worked to rescue children from moral danger, but the age of consent was only raised from 12 to 13 in 1865. The Society for the Prevention of Cruelty to Children was only established in 1891 – 67 years after the one to prevent cruelty to animals.

MARY ELLEN'S ORDEAL

The first case of child abuse officially documented in the United States had to be reported in 1874 to an animal welfare agency. Mary Ellen Wilson's working mother boarded her with a woman when the girl was nearly two. When she could no longer pay, the woman turned Mary Ellen over to New York City's charity department. They allowed another couple, Mary McCormack and her husband, to adopt the girl and then told her real mother she had died.

McCormack, a cruel woman living in Manhattan, would beat the child night and day with anything at hand, including scissors and a rawhide whip. Mary Ellen was not allowed outside and when her mother went to work was chained in a small closet. This torture went on for more than seven years as Mrs McCormack beat, burned, cut and starved the girl. Neighbours could hear her screaming all day, but nothing was done until a case investigator, Etta Wheeler, saw her with scars on her face and arms. She went to authorities who refused to intervene, saying Mary Ellen's unfortunate situation was better than taking her from her mother.

Above: Poor Victorian children often suffered physical and sexual abuse, with nowhere to turn for help.

Right: Henry Bergh founded a society to end animal cruelty in 1866 after visiting Britain and seeing one there.

Mrs Wheeler then contacted Henry Bergh, founder of the American Society for the Prevention of Cruelty to Animals, since there was no law against protecting children from physical abuse. He sent an agent to the neighbourhood to confirm the cruelties, and New York State's Supreme Court removed Mary Ellen from her mother's custody. The 10-year-old girl testified in court in 1874, drawing the *New York Times* headline 'Inhuman Treatment for a Little Waif'. Mrs McCormack received five years of hard labour.

This case inspired a crusade against child abuse and the establishment that year of the New York Society for the Prevention of Cruelty to Children, supposedly the world's first such organization. Mary Ellen was sent to live happily with Mrs Wheeler and her mother. She eventually married, had children and lived to the age of 92, dying in 1956.

> THE NEW YORK SOCIETY FOR THE PREVENTION OF CRUELTY TO CHILDREN WAS SUPPOSEDLY THE WORLD'S FIRST SUCH ORGANIZATION.

CRIMINAL ABORTIONS

To be unmarried and pregnant in the Victorian era was considered the end of a woman's virtue and reputation. Abortion was used to prevent such humiliation and for birth control by working women and those in the middle class wishing to limit their families. Parliament, however, passed the 1861 Offences Against the Person Act (still on the books) that made it illegal for a woman to terminate her own pregnancy. The penalty for her and anyone assisting, including a doctor, was life in prison. Despite this, abortions were very common, with some being labelled as miscarriages. Even doctors were allowed to perform 'therapeutic abortions' for married women when pregnancy threatened their lives.

The infamous back-street abortions were usually induced by

Opposite: While women from better families could receive proper abortions, the poor had to rely on dangerous back-street practitioners.

THE PHYSICIANS' CRUSADE

HORATIO ROBINSON STORER, a Boston surgeon, was a fiery campaigner against abortion. He started the Physicians' Crusade Against Abortion that led to anti-abortion laws in almost every state. It was generally believed that life began at 'quickening', when a mother first felt movements of the foetus (about the fourth month), but Storer argued that life began earlier. He also used the fear of the United States being overrun by migrants if abortions lowered the birth rate of native-born whites. 'This is a question our women must answer', he said in 1868. 'Upon their loins depends the future destiny of the nation'.

injecting water into the uterus. Worse methods involved knitting needles and other sharp instruments. Rough activities often worked, such as riding, running or even taking falls. Eating or drinking a herb, drug or dangerous substance such as turpentine were quicker though often just as painful, and even fatal. In Sheffield in the 1890s, abortions were caused by lead poisoning from water pipes, and this quickly inspired a lead compound marketed for that purpose.

After an abortion, a poor woman sometimes turned to the black market to sell her dead foetus. Anatomists were eager for bodies to dissect and would pay for a foetus that had resulted from abortion, miscarriage or even infanticide.

A woman's place was in the home throughout the nineteenth century. She had the very best role model in Queen Victoria, who stressed happy family life, motherhood and respectability. For these virtues, women were romanticized and idolized. Their restricted lives began to change, however, with the Industrial Revolution, which created concern for those who laboured in awful conditions and those left unemployed and destitute. Especially in cities, women began to leave their homes to do charitable work, and their entry into the real and rough world prompted the beginnings of the feminist movement. In his novel *Bleak House* (1853), Charles Dickens satirized female activists with the characters of Mrs Jellyby and Mrs Pardiggle, who neglected their families for charity work.

Britain's feminist movement became organized in 1859 with the Langham Place Circle in London, formed of middle-class women who campaigned for proper education and employment for women. Several members, including the artist and activist Barbara Leigh Smith, began the first campaign for women's suffrage in 1866. Emmeline Pankhurst, whose husband actively supported votes for women, founded the Women's Franchise League in 1889. New Zealand

MRS. EMMELINE PANKHURST

Above: Emmeline Pankhurst campaigned for women's vote for 40 years and saw the voting equality act passed weeks before her death

had become the first democracy in the world to grant women the vote in 1893, but this right would come later in Britain in 1918 and the United States in 1920. Pankhurst in 1903 would help found the militant Women's Social and Political Union, whose members were the first to be called 'suffragettes'.

CHICAGO GAMBLERS

Among the hard-working and moralistic Victorians, gambling was considered an addictive vice. Often invisible to respectable London families, it was more difficult to control in the young American cities. Chicago soon became a centre of illegal gambling for cards and dice and such sports as boxing, horseracing and cockfighting. By the 1830s, objections by church groups activated city officials to crack down on two gambling dens and jail their proprietors. By 1850, however, some 100 gambling houses existed in the city centre, many of them connected to saloons. Little was done to close these establishments, since they contributed to Chicago's economy through rents, salaries of employees and gambling customers spending in nearby businesses. During the Civil War (1861–65), gamblers from the struggling South moved into Chicago's richer fields, joining Union soldiers around the card and dice tables. The winners were often seen riding in an open carriage with a consort, normally from a bordello.

Gambling dens had progressed into large houses and in 1870 these began

SUSAN B. ANTHONY

FROM HER HOME NEAR Rochester, New York, Anthony campaigned to abolish slavery and support temperance before she became an early crusader for women's right to vote in the United States. She voted illegally in the 1872 presidential election and was arrested, convicted and given a fine she refused to pay. In 1888, Anthony helped establish the International Council on Women and in 1892 became president of the National American Woman Suffrage Association. 'There never will be complete equality,' she said, 'until women themselves make laws and elect lawmakers'. She was the first woman depicted on US currency when her image appeared on a new dollar coin in 1979.

Above: Susan B. Anthony also campaigned for women to own their own property and keep their earnings.

Above: Casinos and other gambling dens in Chicago drew a mixed crowd of rough characters and the city's elite.

to link up as big syndicates. They became strong enough to influence politicians by contributions and keep the police away with payoffs. Soon three syndicates controlled gambling, and violence was used to keep control. Chicago, however, was not immune to the Victorian sense of morality, and campaigns by the public and press forced politicians to close down the city's more obvious gambling organizations. In the 1890s, casinos moved to the suburbs beyond the control of the city.

NEW YORK'S DRAFT RIOTS

The Victorian era coincided with the American Civil War, producing tension and violence in New York City. On 13 July 1863, one of the deadliest riots in American history began when thousands in Manhattan went on a five-day rampage of murder and looting as they reacted to the new law of conscription into the Union army. Since the war was against slave states, the white residents targeted blacks whose cause of freedom they blamed for the war. The city also supported the Southern cause in many ways because of strong economic links to Southern products, especially cotton, which made up 40 per cent of shipping from

New York. If the slaves were freed, there was a fear they would flood the city with cheap labour. New Yorkers had voted strongly against Abraham Lincoln in the 1860 presidential election, and Mayor Fernando Wood even made an unsuccessful proposal that the city itself should secede.

THE VICTIMS WERE MURDERED, MUTILATED AND THEIR BODIES DRAGGED THROUGH THE STREETS TO BE HUNG FROM LAMPPOSTS.

The victims were murdered, mutilated and their bodies dragged through the streets to be hung from lampposts. The official death count was 119, but locals said it had been twice that or more. The mob, often inspired by Irish labourers opposed to African Americans taking their jobs, burned down the Colored Orphan Asylum on Fifth Avenue and any place that catered to African Americans, from businesses to rooming houses and bordellos. The riots continued until federal troops arrived, but many African-American families fled the city forever.

IRISH MOLLIE

ONE OF CHICAGO'S richest and best-dressed gamblers was a Virginian, George Trussell. His special love was Mollie Cosgriff, whom he had met as a 14-year-old chambermaid, and they had a child out of wedlock. Mollie then became the madam, known as 'Irish Mollie', at a brothel.

When the Civil War ended, Trussell purchased a famous trotting horse, Dexter. As Trussell spent more time at his stables, Mollie became lonely. This came to a head in 1866 when he asked her to host a champagne dinner to celebrate one of Dexter's victories. Mollie dutifully invited guests and was humiliated when Trussell failed to attend. Still wearing her white dinner gown, she tracked him down in a saloon, where he stood at the bar. Mollie hugged him and pulled a handgun from her purse, shooting the 32-year-old gambler in the heart. 'George!' she shrieked, 'Have I killed you?' When the police arrived, she begged to kiss Trussell one last time, saying 'I gave up all for him'.

Mollie was charged with murder. Her gun had inexplicably disappeared, and her lawyer pleaded 'temporary emotional insanity'. She served a few months in jail before being pardoned. She moved to California where, ironically, a horse was named after her.

EUROPEAN REVOLUTIONS IN 1848

REPUBLICAN IDEALS FUELLED SEVERAL failed revolts against monarchies in 1848. The first arose in Sicily in January, followed the next month in France, then Austria and Germany. Outbreaks were centred in Paris, Vienna and Berlin. In France, the Second Republic was established, but workers were unsatisfied and rose up in June. Armies in the various countries quickly defeated the revolutionaries in Paris, Prague, Vienna, Berlin and Rome. Strong monarchies were established in Germany, Austria and Italy, and by 1852 the former president of France's Second Republic was named Emperor Napoleon III. Positive results from the revolutions included the start of unification movements in Germany and Italy.

SLAUGHTER IN PARIS

After France's 1871 defeat in the Franco–Prussian war, a furious disagreement arose over what form the new government should take. In general elections in February that year, the country elected a conservative National Assembly, but Parisians, fearing it would try to restore the monarchy, voted for radical republicans. Fearing the worst, the government sent troops to remove cannons from the city. Republicans convinced the troops to join them and shot two generals. As wealthy families fled Paris, the rebels formed their own government, *La Commune*, which represented republican and socialist ideals. Charles Dickens would have approved of their program, which included feeding and housing the poor and limiting the working day to 10 hours.

IN THE 'BLOODY WEEK' THAT FOLLOWED, THE FRENCH ARMY KILLED SOME 20,000 REBELS WHILE LOSING ABOUT 750 OF THEIR OWN.

Communes elected in other cities such as Toulouse, Lyon and Marseille were quickly suppressed, but the Paris Commune organized a resistance against the National Assembly that was meeting in Versailles. On 21 May, government troops were sent through the city to clean out the opposition. The Communards set up barricades in the streets, burned the City Hall, Palace of Justice and Tuileries Palace, and pulled down a statue of

Napoleon. In the 'bloody week' that followed (21–28 May), the French army killed some 20,000 rebels while losing about 750 of their own. With the defeat of the Commune, the government arrested some 38,000 of its members, imprisoned about 10,000 and deported more than 7000 to labour camps in New Caledonia in the South Pacific.

Above: Rebels in the Paris Commune set up solid barricades in 1871, but the French army brutally crushed their movement.

ATTEMPTS ON VICTORIA'S LIFE

Unlike Europe, Britain avoided a serious insurrection during Victoria's reign. The queen was beloved by her subjects but still suffered eight attempted assassinations, more than any other monarch. The first occurred on 10 June 1840, when Edward Oxford, 18, fired twice at the pregnant queen riding with Albert in their open carriage in Hyde Park. He missed and the crowd took him down. Next, on 29 May 1842, John Francis pointed his pistol at the couple in their carriage, but it failed to fire, and he disappeared into Green Park. The following day, he made another attempt, but the shot missed and police quickly arrested him. Five weeks later, on 3 July, John William Bean, 17, attempted a shot at the queen's carriage on the Mall but the gun failed to fire; he escaped but was arrested at home. On 19 June 1849, John Hamilton, an Irish immigrant, fired at the queen as she rode with three of her children, but he used only gunpowder in his weapon. A year later, on 27 June 1850, Robert Pate, known for his mental problems, approached the queen's carriage and struck her on the forehead with his cane, giving her a bruise and a black eye. On 29 February 1872, Arthur O'Connor, 17, climbed the fence at Buckingham Palace and raised his pistol a foot from the queen in the courtyard, but her personal servant, John Brown, tackled him. On 2 March 1882, another mentally disturbed man, Roderick Maclean, shot at the queen as she rode from Windsor's train station, and was restrained by boys from Eton College until arrested.

Below: Queen Victoria escaped assassination on the Wednesday evening of 10 June 1840 when Edward Oxford's two shots went awry.

THE QUEEN'S PROTECTOR

JOHN BROWN, Victoria's manservant who saved her from one assassination, was her confidant after her husband Albert died in 1861. The gruff, bearded Scotsman accompanied her publicly everywhere during their 20-year relationship, acting as a barrier to the dangers on London's streets as they took carriage rides together, with Brown wearing his kilt. He even slept in a room next to her bedroom. Rumours were rife in court circles that they were conducting an affair, even that they had gone to Switzerland in 1868 to be married.

Above: John Brown brought Queen Victoria comfort and protection in her later years. The royal household called him 'the queen's stallion'.

When Brown died in 1883, Victoria wrote to one her ministers, saying how much she missed her 'dear faithful friend's strong arm' and added: 'Perhaps never in history was there so strong and true an attachment, so warm and loving friendship between the sovereign and servant... Strength of character as well as power of frame – the most fearless uprightness, kindness, sense of justice, honesty, independence and unselfishness combined with a tender warm heart...made him one of the most remarkable men'. When the queen died, she left instructions that a lock of Brown's hair be placed in her coffin, along with his photograph, handkerchief and some letters. Mementos of Albert were also buried with her.

The punishments varied greatly depending on the assassins' mental attitudes, with some held in asylums or transported. John Francis was given the most sever sentence of being hanged, drawn and quartered, but Victoria commuted this to banishment for life. She was philosophical about the attacks, saying, 'It is worth being shot at to see how much one is loved'.

2

MIND AND BODY

Victorians experienced some of the city's worse epidemics, but also made good advances in medicine and urban cleanliness. Mental conditions remained misunderstood and treatment was primitive until the latter part of the nineteenth century.

THIS WAS a time when city populations were virtually helpless against a wide range of diseases. Even if the sources could be identified, governments were often slow or unable to act. London finally took action after virulent cholera epidemics struck in 1848–49, killing 14,137, and in 1853, when 10,738 died. Politicians made sure the city's cesspools were cleaned and sewers rebuilt to form a system that remains today. Other British cities suffered the same fate, with an outbreak in Newcastle-upon-Tyne in 1854. Cholera also raged in the United States, with epidemics in 1832 in New York City and in Cincinnati, Ohio.

Overcrowded cities in other countries brought together new victims of a variety of diseases. The bubonic plague was a constant worldwide fear, ravaging populations in China, Japan, India, Iran and Egypt. Smallpox epidemics hit the United States,

Opposite: Dinnertime at a men's workhouse where paupers and the elderly received moral and religious instructions as well as food.

Right: The sketch represents the cholera disease as death pumping water that may be contaminated with sewage.

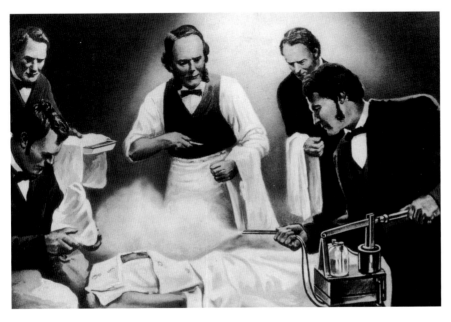

Canada, Australia, South Africa, Ethiopia and Sudan. Yellow fever was responsible for many deaths in southern US cities such as New Orleans and Memphis. Victorian doctors struggled to cure diseases and contain epidemics. Writing in 1838 about tuberculosis, 'a dread disease', Charles Dickens said it was one that 'medicine never cured' and 'wealth never warded off'. Progress was being made on several fronts, however. The French chemist Louis Pasteur in the 1850s found that microorganisms caused infections and disease, then developed vaccinations and the process now known as pasteurization. These discoveries in 1867 led the British surgeon Joseph Lister to first use antiseptics. The German physician Robert Koch determined the bacterial causes of cholera and tuberculosis in the 1880s, with a vaccine for cholera being developed in 1892. An understanding and the treatment of typhus, tetanus and the plague also followed. In 1895, German physicist Wilhelm Röntgen discovered X-rays, which would transform medical diagnoses.

Below: The British surgeon Joseph Lister (centre) watches an assistant using his sterilizing carbolic acid spray.

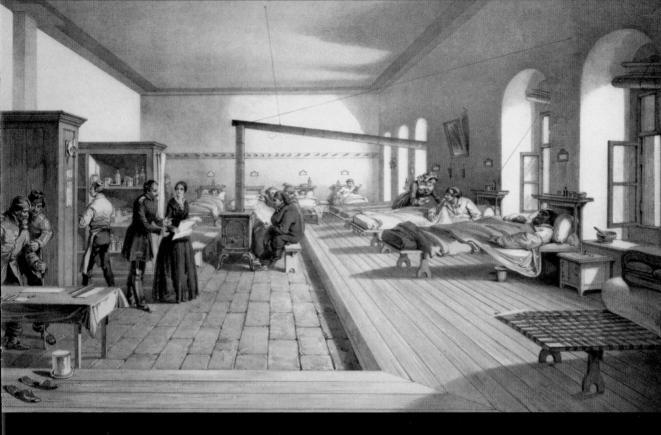

VICTORIANS AT RISK

In 1858, London was the world's most populous city, with about 2,320,000 inhabitants. The average life expectancy of a middle-class man was 45, and a child with luck would reach the age of five. People facing an array of diseases blamed 'miasma' – bad air whose noxious vapours could be detected by an unpleasant smell. This belief was subscribed to by doctors and nurses, including Florence Nightingale, who luckily concluded that thorough cleaning and fresh air would eliminate the smell and disease. She believed hospitals created their own miasma and insisted on airy wards and open balconies. Quack doctors on the streets had a different treatment for the poor, selling medicated vapours to 'cure' consumption (tuberculosis).

The vapour theory was wrong, but it highlighted the city's foul atmosphere, which promoted diseases. Cholera epidemics devastated London in 1848–49 and 1853. The 'Great Stink' in

Above: Florence Nightingale is shown during the Crimean War in the Barrack Hospital at Scutari where she began her hygiene campaign.

the oppressive summer of 1858 forced parliamentarians to fund a massive engineering project to build an 83-mile (133-kilometre) new sewer system. It diverted foul water from the old system into new lower-level sewers. These pipes ran along both sides of the Thames to send sewage to new treatment works east of London where it was pumped into the sea.

One did not have to leave home to be in danger. Many Victorians were poisoned by arsenic used in green dyes for their wallpaper. A Birmingham doctor, William Hinds, warned in 1857 about the pigment, saying, 'A great deal of slow poisoning

Below: Depicted are the potential hazards of a Victorian household, including arsenic, rats, cockroaches, thick smoke and even pages of taxes and bills to be paid.

is going on in Great Britain'. Queen Victoria had the green wallpaper in Buckingham Palace stripped off after a visiting dignitary became ill. The famed wallpaper designer William Morris disagreed, calling the arsenic scare an example of hysteria (because his family's arsenic mine was a leading producer). The poisonous dye was also used for clothes and children's toys. Indeed, arsenic was everywhere in the house, used as a powder in cosmetics, to remove unwanted hair and to kill rats and flies (as well as spouses).

THERE WAS THE COMPETITION OF WORKING HORSES, ABOUT 300,000 IN THE 1890S, WHO CONTRIBUTED AT LEAST 1000 TONNES OF DUNG EACH DAY TO THE ALREADY FILTHY STREETS.

WALKING LONDON STREETS

Strolling through London during Victoria's reign was seldom a pleasure. First, there was the competition of working horses, about 300,000 in the 1890s, who contributed at least 1000 tonnes of dung each day to the already filthy streets. Loose pigs and sheep added their share. Young boys were employed to dodge vehicles and scoop it up immediately, but this was a mission impossible. Horse urine also soaked the streets. Refuse collectors with horse-drawn carts made haphazard visits and generally expected tips to remove rubbish left outside houses. In the slums, the problem increased when some residents defecated over street grates rather than in their filthy privies. Describing an area near Notting Hill, Charles Dickens's own weekly magazine, *Household Words*, wrote in 1859: 'There are foul ditches, open sewers, and defective drains, smelling most offensively' and 'all is charged with putrescent matter'.

THE PROBLEM WITH CESSPOOLS

The Victorian cesspool was a small brick septic tank dug about six feet deep and four feet wide (1.8 by 1.2 metres). It would be set away from the house in rural areas, but London and other crowded cities had to squeeze them into the basements of every house. Right above was the family's privy, and this basic arrangement worked, although it was accompanied by the smell.

JOSEPH BAZALGETTE

Left: Construction of the Fleet Street sewer was a major project that today remains in surprisingly good condition.

THE THAMES WAS VIRTUALLY an open sewer for water-flushing toilets when Joseph Bazalgette was appointed as chief engineer for London's new Metropolitan Board of Works in 1856. To overcome the 'Great Stink' of 1858, he built 1,100 miles (1,770 kilometres) of street sewers to drain off the raw filth; below those he used 318 million bricks to construct 83 miles (133 kilometres) of sewers. They directed the flow into the river, where tides conveyed it to the sea.

The first phase was completed in 1865, but cholera returned the next year. The system still dumped tons of raw sewage into the river. In 1878 a pleasure boat sank near an outflow and 640 passengers died, many poisoned by Thames sewage. Bazalgette corrected the problem by a series of treatment plants. With this addition, the system enormously reduced Londoners' illness and death rates, and the dreaded cholera was eradicated.

Bazalgette's most revolutionary scheme was to create the Thames Embankments, named Victoria, Albert and Chelsea, to hold the sewers running along the river.

This narrowed the Thames by 50 yards (45 metres) and created a cleansing rush of water. Queen Victoria knighted Bazalgette for his work, then the largest civil engineering project in the world. Opened in 1885, it had taken nearly 20 years to complete.

The design was porous so liquid waste could seep out and leave the rest. This was taken away by 'night soil men', who by law could not begin work until midnight. The crew's 'rope man' lowered a tub or wicker basket to the 'hole man' who had climbed down into the pit and had the worst job of shovelling the excrement into the container. This was taken by two 'tub men' to their cart to be sold to farmers as manure. The crew's hard work was prone to accidents and the fumes caused disease or even death by suffocation.

Trouble with the system arrived when water closets became popular in the mid-nineteenth century. It seemed reasonable to connect them to the existing cesspools, but flushing so much water resulted in an overflow of waste below. Foul-smelling liquid soaked the basements. Then the stench became unbearable, seeping into every room, while the rising air brought with it diseases such as cholera and typhoid. Relief would eventually come when toilets were connected directly to the sewers.

Below: This *Punch* magazine cartoon from 1852 shows a crowd around a pile of rubbish in the street – a breeding ground for cholera.

'KING CHOLERA'

Outbreaks of cholera have killed people throughout history. In 1832, five years before Victoria became queen, it hit the United Kingdom, killing 6536 in London and more than 55,000 overall. Called 'King Cholera', the disease returned with a vengeance in 1848–49, causing 14,137 deaths in London. In 1853, cholera killed 10,738 in the city and some 52,000 others in England and Wales.

This was only part of the worldwide pandemic beginning in 1852 that would see Russia suffer more than a million deaths. Millions more died in

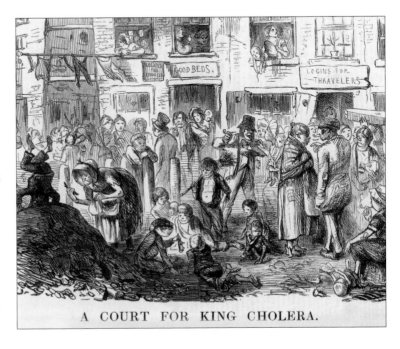

A COURT FOR KING CHOLERA.

China, Japan, India, Korea, the Philippines, Iraq, Iran, Tunisia, the USA and other countries as the disease moved around the globe throughout the Victoria era.

Cholera was a feared disease that caused diarrhoea, vomiting, stomach cramps, pain in the limbs and severe dehydration, and could kill within hours of the symptoms appearing. Physicians believed it came from 'miasmic' conditions that particularly affected those who were physically and even morally weak. Haphazard treatments involved bleeding and taking opium. Many fraudulent medicine men sold preparations often based on brandy, such as Rymer's Peruvian Tonic Drops.

The true source – a microscopic organism – was discovered in 1883 by the German doctor Robert Koch, showing that the disease was contagious. A London physician, John Snow, had come to the same conclusion in 1854 by practical means. Noting that a cholera outbreak in the Soho district had killed more than 500 people in 10 days, he traced the incidents to a pump in Broad Street and had authorities remove the handle. The fatalities immediately fell. As officials began to blame household waste and told Londoners to remove dung heaps and liquid filth from houses, the residents dumped their cesspools and other raw sewage into the Thames, making things worse. By 1885, London's new sewage system brought about a safer city, while Russian doctor Waldemar Haffkine developed a cholera vaccine in 1892.

Below: Robert Koch discovered the bacteria that causes cholera and received the 1905 Nobel Prize for Physiology or Medicine.

TUBERCULOSIS

Tuberculosis, then called consumption, reached epidemic levels in the mid-1800s in Britain, Europe and the United States. Airborne and highly contagious, it killed seven family members of the Victorian novelist Charlotte Brontë. TB thrived in the conditions of Charles Dickens's London, especially among the poor, who were suffering from malnutrition and living in overcrowded neighbourhoods in poorly ventilated houses. Between 1851 and 1910, about four million people in England and Wales died of consumption, including 50 per cent of those aged 20 to 24.

CHOLERA WAS A FEARED DISEASE THAT CAUSED DIARRHOEA, VOMITING, STOMACH CRAMPS, PAIN IN THE LIMBS AND SEVERE DEHYDRATION.

Without antibiotics, victims of the terrible lung disease slowly wasted away, confined to sanatoriums. Victorians called the disease 'the white plague' because of the pale skin of its victims, a look that was romanticized by Victorian writers. When Virginia, the wife of American writer Edgar Allan Poe was dying of the disease, he described her as being 'delicately, morbidly angelic'. Others thought victims looked as if they had been bitten by vampires.

TB had no real treatment in the nineteenth century. Doctors bled and purged patients, advising them to rest and seek clean air and a healthier climate, as in the mountains. As with cholera, they believed the disease was caused by miasmas until 1882, when Robert Koch found the bacterium that was responsible. (Koch, who had also discovered the bacterium that caused cholera – see above, was awarded the Noble Prize in Medicine in 1905.) This discovery produced a new treatment to contain TB, along with a campaign to stop people spitting in public

THE HYDROELECTRIC CHAIN

IN 1870, AFTER SUFFERING leg pains, Charles Dickens ordered the latest fad to cure pain: the electrified Pulvermacher belt. The device, sold by the physicist Isaac Pulvermacher, used a belt of batteries soaked in vinegar and connected to electrodes on the skin. Introduced at the Great Exhibition of 1851 in London's Crystal Palace, this electrotherapy device was used by some 50,000 people in Europe and America. It sent a tingling current or slight shock over an area of their body and could supposedly cure a range of problems, including depression, fatigue, headaches, heart palpitations, haemorrhoids and diarrhoea.

and placing the victims in well-aired sanatoriums for months or years. Between 1860 and 1895, England and Wales saw a 39 per cent reduction in consumption deaths, although it was only in 1946 that the antibiotic streptomycin was proven to cure the disease.

VICTORIAN DRUGS

Substance abuse in Victorian times was an easy path to take in countries around the world. British chemist shops sold drugs without restrictions until the Pharmacy Act of 1868, and they remained commonly available after that. Drugs were used by all classes of society and were generally considered a habit, not an addition. Alcohol was also a common ingredient in medicines, even for kidney and liver complaints.

Below: Leadbeater's Laudanum, which also was 47 percent alcohol, became a popular product in the United States in the late 1800s.

Laudanum, an opium derivative mixed with water or wine, was the most popular, being taken daily as a painkiller in households for almost any complaint, from coughs to heart disease. It was popular with writers such as Samuel Taylor Coleridge, who wrote his famous poem 'Kubla Kahn' (published in 1816) after an intense dream he had after taking laudanum. Other takers included Charles Dickens, Elizabeth Barrett Browning, George Eliot, Lord Byron, Percy Bysshe Shelly and Bram Stoker.

Opium became readily available from the far corners of the British Empire and developed a romantic image. In 1821, Thomas De Quincey had written his famous book *Confessions of an English Opium-Eater*, praising its effect on the creative powers. Opium was also sold as a universal cure in a variety of mixtures and in such patented medicines as Mother's Friend, which was given to children to calm and sometimes kill them. The dismal opium dens of East London were less romantic. Oscar Wilde described their sadness in his 1891 novel *The Picture of Dorian Gray*: 'There were opium dens where one could buy oblivion, dens of

CShCAINE
TOOTHACHE DROPS
Instantaneous Cure!
PRICE 15 CENTS.
Prepared by the
LLOYD MANUFACTURING CO.
219 HUDSON AVE., ALBANY, N. Y.
For sale by all Druggists.

horror where the memory of old sins could be destroyed by the madness of sins that were new'.

Cocaine was sold in medicines advertised to alleviate indigestion and to stop vomiting while pregnant and was taken in drops and lozenges for colds and toothaches. A French wine, Vin Mariani, was made with coca leaves and drunk to restore health, winning the approval of Queen Victoria and Rudyard Kipling among many others. Even the household authority Mrs Beeton recommended it as a home remedy in her 1861 book *Mrs Beeton's Household Management*, but warned against addiction.

Morphine was found in many products, including Mrs Winslow's

Above: Cocaine was also used to numb pain by wrapping a tooth with a cotton ball soaked in the drug.

Left: Mrs Winslow's Soothing Syrup was nicknamed 'the baby killer', with thousands of children believed to have died from overdoses.

CURES DYSENTERY AND DIARRHŒA.
MRS. WINSLOW'S
WILL RELIEVE GRIPING IN THE BOWELS.
INSTANTLY CURES WIND COLIC.
SOOTHING SYRUP
FOR CHILDREN.
JEREMIAH CURTIS & SON. NEW YORK.

THE TAPEWORM DIET

FAD DIETS BECAME BIG business in the nineteenth century. Some Victorian women believed they would lose weight by swallowing tapeworm capsules that would mature in their intestines and consume food. After the desired weight loss, you could take a pill to kill the tapeworm, which was eventually passed (with some side effects). This unpleasant diet was advertised without mentioning that the tapeworm could grow to 30 feet (9 metres) and cause diseases such as epilepsy and meningitis.

Other unusual Victorian diets included 'miracle' arsenic pills and a daily drink of vinegar, a regimen followed by Lord Byron despite the resulting diarrhoea and vomiting.

Soothing Syrup, advertised to cure teething troubles in infants, and Dr Seth Arnold's Cough Killer, to cure everything from coughs to malaria.

AN UNHEALTHY FASHION

Victorian women suffered through several types of painful clothes before finding some comfort at the end of the century. The early wide bell-shaped crinoline hoop skirts were clumsy and also dangerous when the flammable fabric was near open fireplaces. They were worn with six or more petticoats made of horsehair or stiffened with cane – a heavy load to bear. More pain came with the tight boned corset designed to create a tiny waist; it also often created fainting spells and a deformity of the spine and ribs. A further danger was the popularity of emerald-green arsenic dyes. *The British Medical Journal* described the Victorian woman: 'She actually carries in her skirts poison enough to slay the whole of the admirers she may meet with in half a dozen ball-rooms'.

By 1870, this fashion gave way to a flattened look in front but an enormous soft bustle behind, replaced in 1883 by the hard version. This humped shape was intended to emphasize a small waist and continue a curve from the bosom. These disappeared in the mid-1890s with the popularity of long flared skirts

Opposite: The crinoline became so popular, in 1862 a London company employed 2000 workers producing 4000 crinoline metal cages a day.

Above: Women confined to a workhouse lived in crowded close quarters, even when consuming their poor quality meals.

and narrow waists. Younger women adopted a more casual style; the more daring even wore bloomers suited to their active lives, which now included bicycles. This end of Victorian fashion is considered a major step towards feminine liberation.

POOR FOOD FOR THE POOR

Slum dwellers in Victorian times were undernourished, existing on food that caused a variety of health problems. Families survived mainly on bread, porridge, broth made from boiled bones, and tea. Other regular fare included dripping fat, sheep trotters, offal, tripe, potato parings and rotten vegetables. Tainted meat like broxy (diseased sheep) was sometimes added. Few among the poor had ovens and had to eat cold meals or cook over an open fire with perhaps one pot also used for the baby's bath. Such a weak diet caused children to develop anaemia and rickets, and this stunted their growth.

Things were worse for anyone confined in a workshop or prison. Meals sometimes had a portion of stringy meat but no vegetables. The usual fare was stale bread, slops and skilly, a thin gruel or soup. In prisons until 1842, bad meals were considered a proper form of punishment. New inmates were given a period of 'scientific starvation' to weaken their aggression and discourage poor people from offending just to receive prison meals.

All this contrasted with those in more comfortable families, whose diet consisted of meat, good vegetables and fresh milk. Because meals were without sugar (highly taxed until the 1870s) and processed food, their diet was healthier than our modern one. An exception was Queen Victoria, who could consume seven courses in less than 30 minutes.

BOMBAY'S PLAGUE

In 1896, the bubonic plague hit the overcrowded city of Bombay (now Mumbai), India. Officials recorded 3148 deaths between October that year and January 1897. The city's population of some 850,000 was reduced by about half when many families fled, spreading the disease outside the city.

The plague had struck Hong Kong in 1894 and had probably spread from there. The British Indian government resorted to colonial state power to introduce harsh restrictions to control the epidemic, including forced evacuations, quarantines, segregation camps for families of victims, travel restrictions and hospitalization. These measures were greatly resented by the locals and led to riots. Some Indians did not trust Western medicine, with rumours warning that doctors wished to poison patients in order to experiment on them and to extract a valuable oil from the bodies.

When the plague spread to cities such as Calcutta (now Kolkata), Karachi and Pune, and then into the countryside, the government took a softer approach, bringing in Indian medical practices and urging inoculation that was not compulsory. A Russian doctor, Waldemar Haffkine (see box), had rushed to Bombay and quickly developed a plague vaccine that worked.

INDIA'S PIONEERING DOCTOR

ANANDIBAI JOSHEE, 18, left India in 1883 to become the first Indian woman to study medicine in the United States. She wrote to America's Presbyterian Church for help but was refused because she would not convert from Hinduism to Christianity. Nevertheless, she won support from the Hindu community and sold her own jewellery to pay for her studies. She enrolled at the Women's Medical College of Pennsylvania and graduated in 1886. Sadly, she contracted tuberculosis before graduating and died in India the next year, aged 21. Her dream had ended, but Joshee inspired many Indian women to become doctors.

Above: Anandi Joshi (left) was married when nine to a widower 20 years older who encouraged her medical studies in America.

'A SAVIOUR OF HUMANITY'

THE DOCTOR CREDITED WITH saving thousands of Indian people from the plague was a Russian who first made a medical breakthrough in 1892 at the Pasteur Institute in Paris. Waldemar Haffkine developed a cholera vaccine, first testing it on himself. He used it the following year in Calcutta, where he inoculated 45,000 people, and the cholera death rate fell by 70 per cent. While there, he survived an assassination attempt by Islamic extremists.

Haffkine moved to Bombay in 1896, then besieged by the plague; within three months he had produced a vaccine. As with the cholera vaccine, he first injected himself with a dose four times as strong as those he later gave to patients. British authorities welcomed this but were suspicious of Haffkine's closeness to Indians. They rejected his appeals to eliminate the worse restrictions for those he inoculated.

Haffkine left India in 1915 to settle in France. His cholera vaccine was used around the world, including in Russia in 1898, where it saved thousands in his native country, which had spurned him because he was Jewish. In 1925 his institute in Bombay was renamed in his honour. Britain's famous doctor, Joseph Lister, summed up the brilliant Haffkine as 'a saviour of humanity'.

भारत INDIA

Dr. W. M. HAFFKINE
1860 - 1930

INDIA SECURITY PRESS

न.पै.
15
nP

Above: India issued a 1964 commemorative stamp honouring Dr Haffkine on the 104th anniversary of his birth in 1860.

Many locals believed the injections led to impotence, sterility and even death. However, this medical collaboration between the two cultures led to an enduring reorganization of public health in British India.

CHINESE FOOTBINDING

Victorian women in the Western world endured some painful fashions, but Chinese women suffered more for the sake of beauty, status and a good marriage. Small feet were thought to be beautiful and refined, as were small waists in Britain. Female children as young as two, but usually four or five, had their feet broken and tightly bound for their entire lives. All their toes would be broken except the big one and then folded back underneath the sole, so the feet would not grow beyond three inches (7.5 centimetres) (known as the 'golden lotus') or four (10 centimetres) (the 'silver lotus'). Estimates say one in ten girls died from shock. A young girl's foot would sometimes suffer necrosis (tissue death), as seen in frostbite. Besides causing excruciating pain through life, the practice caused infections and back problems from walking on the heels.

Footbinding had begun in the tenth century and continued unabated. In the nineteenth century, up to 50 per cent of Chinese women and virtually all in the upper classes underwent the procedure. Several attempts were made to halt it. In 1874, a British priest in Shanghai and Christian women in Xiamen called for its end, but the practice continued until 1912, when the government banned it. Even then, it took the Communist revolution in 1949 to enforce a ban.

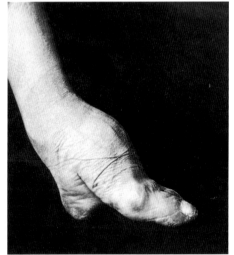

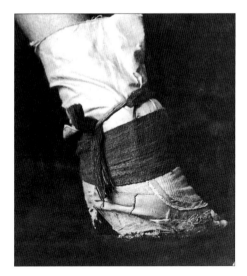

Above: This photograph shows how a bound foot would gradually become deformed over time.

RAISING THE DEAD

With so many deaths each day, Londoners turned to spiritualism and mystics who claimed to contact the departed. Despite the advances of science, most Victorians were superstitious

and believed in the supernatural, paranormal and occult. Séances became especially popular in the 1850s in Britain, Europe and America, although the happenings were riddled with fraud. During a séance, a medium would fall into a trance and reveal the dead person's answers through taps on the table or through his or her own altered voice. In the most elaborate version, the dead person's hands, face and body appeared from behind a curtain. Queen Victoria and Prince Albert first took part in a séance in 1846; others who attempted to speak to the dead through a medium included Mary Todd Lincoln, wife of Abraham Lincoln, Prime Minister William Gladstone, the poet Elizabeth Barrett Browning and the novelist Arthur Conan Doyle.

Victoria herself was convinced that Albert contacted her after his death in 1861. She was amazed when a 13-year-old spiritualist and medium, Robert James Lees, said Albert had contacted him during a séance using Victoria's pet name known only to her late husband. The youth was supposedly invited to Windsor Castle for further séances that contacted Albert. Lees also claimed that his psychic vision had helped the police search for Jack the Ripper.

READING THE HEAD

Advertisements called phrenology 'the only true science of mind'. Many believed phrenologists could inspect the bumps and shapes of a person's skull to discover how separate areas of the brain had developed. This relied on the assumption that

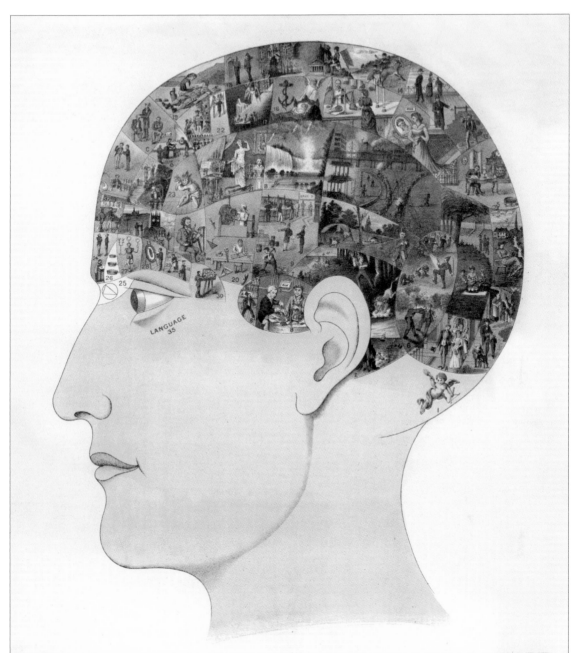

A NEW SYMBOLICAL HEAD AND PHRENOLOGICAL CHART.
WITH THE NAME AND DEFINITION OF EACH ORGAN,
by R. B. D. Wells, Phrenologist, West Bank, Scarbro.

1.—AMATIVENESS. Love between the sexes. *Excess*—Sensuality. *Deficiency*—Coldheartedness.

A.—CONJUGALITY. Desire to marry. *Excess*—Envy towards love rivals. *Def.*—Inconstancy.

2.—PARENTAL LOVE. Love of children, parents, and pets. *Excess*—Pampers and spoils children.

3.—FRIENDSHIP. Social feeling, love of society. *Excess*—Inordinate attachment to friends.

4.—INHABITIVENESS. Love of home, patriotism. *Excess*—Home sickness. *Def.*—Neglect of home.

5.—CONTINUITY. Concentration of thought, application. *Excess*—Prolixity. *Def.*—Love of variety.

E.—VITATIVENESS. Attachment to life. *Excess*—Dread of death. *Def.*—Desire for death.

6.—COMBATIVENESS. Pluck, boldness,
courage, defence. *Excess*—Quarrelsomeness and love of conflict.

7.—DESTRUCTIVENESS. Propelling force, energy. *Excess*—Tendency to destroy, cruelty, malice, revenge.

8.—ALIMENTIVENESS. Relish for food. *Excess*—Gluttony, drunkenness. *Def.*—Little desire for food.

9.—ACQUISITIVENESS. Desire to earn money, trade, economise and accumulate. *Excess*—Avarice, selfishness.

10.—SECRETIVENESS. Policy, reserve, self-control. *Excess*—Evasion, cunning. *Def.*—Frankness, bluntness.

11.—CAUTIOUSNESS. Anxiety, guardedness, hesitancy. *Excess*—Indecision, fear. *Def.*—Indiscretion.

12.—APPROBATIVENESS. Desire for popularity, ambition, display. *Excess*—Affectation, vanity. *Def.*—Lack of politeness.

13.—SELF-ESTEEM. Independence, authority, dignity. *Excess*—Egotism. *Def.*—Servility.

14.—FIRMNESS. Stability, tenacity of will, decision. *Excess*—Obstinacy. *Def.*—Fickleness.

15.—CONSCIENTIOUSNESS. Circumspection, integrity, justice. *Excess*—Undue self-condemnation. *Def.*—Inconsistency.

16.—HOPE. Speculation, cheerfulness, hope in a future state. *Excess*—Castle building.

17.—SPIRITUALITY. Impressibility, trust, faith. *Excess*—Superstition. *Def.*—Scepticism.

18.—VENERATION.—Defence, worship, antiquity. *Excess*—Idolatry, bigotry.

19.—BENEVOLENCE. Sympathy, liberality, kindness. *Excess*—Prodigality in giving.

20.—CONSTRUCTIVENESS. Contrivance, ingenuity, invention. *Def.*—Inability to use tools.
21.—IDEALITY. Refinement, love of the perfect, poetical sentiment. *Excess*—Fastidiousness. *Def.*—Lack of taste and refinement.

B.—SUBLIMITY. Love of the grand, sublime, and terrific. *Excess*—Bombast. *Def.*—Cannot appreciate the sublime.

22.—IMITATION. Power to copy, to draw, imitate, and mimic. *Excess*—Buffoonery.

23.—MIRTHFULNESS. Wit, humour, sense of the comic. *Excess*—Ill-timed ridicule. *Def.*—Cannot appreciate mirth.

24.—INDIVIDUALITY. Power of observation and desire to be an eye witness. *Excess*—Curiosity, and impudent observation.

25.—FORM. Memory of shape, configuration, and faces. *Def.*—Inability to remember form and outlines.

26.—SIZE. Measurement of bulk, proportion, or quantity by the eye. *Excess*—Failure by disproportion.
27.—WEIGHT. Sense of gravity, ability to balance, ride, climb, shoot, &c. *Excess*—Too risky in climbing. *Def.*—Liability to stumble.

28.—COLOUR. Ability to match and compare colours, and evince taste in their arrangement. *Def.*—Colour blind.

29.—ORDER. Neatness, system, method. *Excess*—Too particular and precise. *Def.*—Slovenliness.

30.—CALCULATION. Mental computation, ability to estimate. *Def.*—Inability to reckon.

31.—LOCALITY. Memory of places, desire to travel. *Excess*—Constant roving desire. *Def.*—Forgets places.

32.—EVENTUALITY. Memory of facts, historical records and events. *Def.*—Forgetfulness of facts.

33.—TIME. Memory of dates, punctuality, sense of duration. *Def.*—Forgetfulness of the lapse of time.
34.—TUNE. Love of music, modulation, sense of harmony. *Def.*—Inability to appreciate the concord of sweet sounds.

35.—LANGUAGE. Memory of what is heard, and ability to communicate thoughts and ideas. *Excess*—Loquacity.

36.—CAUSALITY. Philosophical reasoning and planning capacity. *Excess*—Too theoretical. *Def.*—Lack of comprehensiveness.

37.—COMPARISON. Criticism, analysis, the ability to compare and illustrate. *Def.*—Inability to apply knowledge.

C.—HUMAN NATURE. Intuitive insight into character, sagacity, penetration.

D.—AGREEABLENESS. Youthfulness, blandness, suavity. *Def.*—Abruptness of deportment.

THE FOWLER BROTHERS

LORENZO AND ORSON FOWLER did more than anyone to commercialize phrenology. They developed head readings in the 1830s to improve the mind, and sold equipment for this. In their Phrenological Institute in New York City, they collected skulls and published the *American Phrenological Journal*. Lorenzo's wife, Lydia, was the second woman to receive a US medical degree. She also read heads, including those of Charles Dickens and Edgar Allan Poe. The Fowlers opened a London office in 1863. Mark Twain came for a reading using a pseudonym and was told by Lorenzo that one cavity indicated a lack of humour.

Above: Orson Fowler, the older brother, became a believer in phrenology while a student at Amherst College in Massachusetts.

the brain was composed of different 'organs' that controlled certain faculties. The pretentious belief was so strong that some employers demanded readings of candidates' abilities and honesty. Other applications were made for educational prospects and to discover criminal tendencies. Eventually the dubious science was used to 'prove' ethnic and racial differences.

Phrenology first became popular in Britain in the 1820s, then more popular the next decade in America and France and by the 1840s in Germany. Many advocates came from prominent families. The most devoted followers were in the United States, inspired by promoters who said it was possible to strengthen the positive brain organs. According to John van Wyhe, a science historian, the fad of phrenology became unpopular, unfashionable and discredited by later Victorians, who were more aware of the true sciences. Belief lingered on, however, with the British Phrenological Society lasting until 1967.

The sale of unreliable over-the-counter medicines became a big business in America in the later Victorian years. They were sold from travelling medicine shows headed by quacks who titled themselves 'Professor' or even 'Doctor'. Their primary aim was to create diseases rather than cure any. At the least, they brought entertainment to the far reaches of the United States. A typical show provided decent music-hall entertainment to draw crowds around the wagon. This was followed by the showman's pitch to purchase his miracle elixirs for the audience members' ailments and diseases or any he could convince them they had. Some shows became so popular, halls were rented and admission charged. The largest and most successful was the Kickapoo Indian Medicine Company, whose oils were supposed to offer 'quick cures for all pains'. The entertainment included war dances, dog acts, ventriloquists, acrobats and fire eaters. By 1890, the company had employed 800 Indians, making up nearly 100 troupes on the road at the same time.

'Patent' medicines were almost never actually patented. They began in England as 'patents of royal favour' and were exported to the colonies. One great success in both countries was Poor Man's Friend. Americans soon decided it was cheaper to bottle their own. They gave the medicines exotic or descriptive names, such as Wright's Indian Vegetable Pills, which promised to 'remove all obstructions' from the body and 'give vigor and activity to the entire system'. Some patent medicines were legitimate and have survived: Richardson's Croup and Pneumonia Cure Salve is now sold as Vicks VapoRub.

Below: Wright's Indian Vegetable Pills claimed to help pregnant women by 'cleansing the body of morbid conditions'.

WRIGHT'S INDIAN VEGETABLE PILLS Cure all Bilious Complaints

MENTAL ILLNESS

The Victorians classified mental illness into mania, monomania, dementia, melancholia, idiocy and imbecility. They believed the main causes were heredity, environment and weak morals. Of particular concern was the rush of workers to new crowded cities, luring them from the morality of rural family life. Corruption awaited in such temptations as alcohol, drugs and promiscuity, all of which could lead the morally weak into insane asylums. Many were built in the nineteenth century, when the mental patient population rose from some 10,000 to about 100,000. As well as basic treatment, these hospitals were a way of removing people with unacceptable behaviour from public view. Many were 'mad women' suffering from hysteria that doctors linked to sexual problems. Wives' infidelity was sometimes labelled 'moral insanity'.

If two doctors could be persuaded to issue certificates of insanity, anyone could be incarcerated in an asylum. They were run like prisons, and indeed the patients were known as prisoners. Besides the mentally ill, asylums often housed those who were eccentric or just a nuisance to their families. Patients were divided into the curable and incurable. The latter seldom received treatment beyond a bed and food. Terrified patients could be strapped into a chair or bed for most of the day. The Sussex Lunatic Asylum even locked inmates into a large wire 'parrot cage'. Unruly patients in all asylums were beaten, starved, put in straitjackets, isolated and given sedatives like bromides.

When the London Asylum for the Insane opened in 1870, it emphasized moral therapy with the hope of returning patients to society. The program was based on the Victorian values of work, exercise, leisure and a healthy diet. Those with less serious conditions could tend and enjoy the garden. Therapy results were hindered by overcrowding and control by the inspector of prisons that, according to the asylum's superintendent, was 'too unbearably military for endurance'. In 1886 Parliament passed the Idiots Act to separate people with low intelligence from those with true mental problems. Facilities were built for 'the care, education and training of idiots and imbeciles'.

Above: Many Victorians were wrongly committed for insanity, but miserable asylum conditions, often with solitary confinement, could lead to mental problems.

BEDLAM HOSPITAL

'Bedlam' was the popular name for the Bethlehem Royal Hospital, which became infamous for its treatment of those with serious mental problems. Opened in the Bishopsgate ward of London as a general hospital in 1330, it began to admit 'lunatics' in 1403 and became England's first mental institution. Bedlam charged the public for tours to gawk and laugh at the disturbed patients and their antics. The hospital moved to the city's Moorfields area in 1675 and discontinued the tours in 1770. Another move was to St George's Fields in Southwark in 1815. Cruel treatments included patients being beaten, starved, put in straitjackets, chained to the wall and given 'rotational therapy', in which the victim was raised into the air in a chair and spun around for hours.

Many Victorians still regarded the mentally ill as freaks, although the government had ended the hospital's cruel treatments in the early nineteenth century. John Timbs, a commentator in 1867, wrote that 'the management of lunatics has here attained perfection'. However, a woman could still be

Below: Toward the end of the nineteenth century conditions improved for Bedlam's patients who had more space for indoor and outdoor activities.

BEDLAM'S ALIENIST

SIR ALEXANDER MORISON WAS a Victorian doctor of mental illness, a physician then known as an 'alienist'. Born in Edinburgh, he became a pioneer in psychiatry and gave the first formal lectures on the subject. He was inspector of lunatic asylums in Surrey before becoming a physician at the Bethlehem Hospital in 1835. He was knighted three years later. Morison's impressive portrait in the Scottish National Gallery of Art was painted by Richard Dadd, a patient of his in Bedlam who had been confined for murdering his father, believing he was the devil.

locked up for postnatal depression or even because her husband wished to be rid of her. Some of the criminally insane included Edward Oxford, who nearly assassinated Queen Victoria (see Chapter 1), and James Hadfield, confined for 39 years for shooting at George III. Bedlam's inmates were listed as 'prisoners' until 1890, when Parliament changed their status to 'patients'.

WOMEN AND HYSTERIA

Hysteria was the first mental problem attributed only to women. Victorians associated the disorder with fragile female emotions, and many women carried a bottle of smelling salts on an outing in case excitement caused them to feel dizzy or faint. Other symptoms of erratic female behaviour were said to be outbursts, irritability, anxiety, nervousness and erotic fantasies. Victorian ladies were not supposed to enjoy sex, and this led them to sexual frustration. Doctors resorted to 'pelvic massage' to cure their hysteria (the word comes from the Greek for uterus). In the late 1880s, Dr Joseph Mortimer Granville, an English physician, patented an electromechanical vibrator to relieve this type of mental disorder.

The worst cases of immoral or other scandalous behaviours could be recorded as mental illness that often led to the insane asylum. Since Victorians believed that female emotions were connected to women's reproductive organs, doctors in asylums regularly conducted hysterectomies throughout the queen's reign.

FREUD AND HYSTERIA

Although the Austrian neurologist Sigmund Freud became the
twentieth century's most famous psychoanalyst, his first successes
came in the 1890s in treating hysteria. Another Viennese
physician, Josef Breuer, had relieved the symptoms in a female
patient by having her recall earlier unpleasant experiences under
hypnosis. He informed Freud about this and referred patients
to him. Together in 1895 they published *Studien uber Hysteria*
(*Studies on Hysteria*). They later stopped their collaboration
after disagreeing about methods of therapy. Freud saw that most
patients talked without hypnosis, and in 1896 he coined the term
psychoanalysis.

Below: For their joint
publication Freud wrote
four of the five case
studies. The book
received mixed reviews
from psychiatrists.

Treating female hysterics in his clinic, Freud became convinced
that their unconscious thoughts and neurotic symptoms were
caused by repressed sexual urges or experiences. By 1897, he had
concluded that the patients' memories
had not happened but were repressed
childhood fantasies of being seduced by
an adult. Two years later, he published
Die Traumdeutung (*The Interpretation
of Dreams*), suggesting that dreams
were an outlet for people to fulfil their
real desires in an imaginary way.

Many doctors had believed hysteria
was brought about by a woman's lack
of conception and motherhood. Freud
reversed this, saying hysteria caused
such neurotic expressions. He also
decided that this was not just a woman's problem, admitting
he had symptoms of 'my little hysteria' that was made worse by
his work.

A QUEEN IN HIDING

Victoria's world seemed to end with the death of her husband,
Prince Albert, at the age of 42. She blamed their eldest son,
Bertie (later Edward VII), who had bedded a prostitute while
with the army. His parents were devastated, and Albert visited

him for a long talk while walking in the rain. Albert returned ill and three weeks later died of typhus. The sight of her guilty son repelled Victoria, who said, 'I never can or shall look at him without a shudder'.

The queen, also 42, was too grief-stricken to attend Albert's funeral. She wore black mourning clothes for the remainder of her life, 40 years (a year was traditional). She avoided going out to meet her subjects for three years, becoming known as the Widow of Windsor. Prime Minister Benjamin Disraeli coaxed her out, and she reluctantly attended special events, highlighted by her Diamond Jubilee in 1897, celebrating 60 years on the throne. Otherwise, Victoria remained a recluse while maintaining a close relationship with her servant John Brown (see Chapter 1). She changed nothing in the room where Albert died, keeping the glass he had last drunk from by his bed and having maids lay out his clothes daily and change fresh flowers. His other rooms were also kept as shrines.

Some observers, including Members of Parliament, feared that Victoria was insane. Before his death, Albert told her personal physician, Robert Ferguson, 'The Queen has heard that you have paid much attention to mental disease and is afraid she is about to lose her mind. She sees visions and hears sounds and is much troubled as to what will become of her when she is dead. She thinks of worms eating her – and is weeping and wretched'. Ferguson, however, diagnosed her anxiety as 'disorder of her digestive organs'.

Victoria's melancholic nature and deep depression was revealed 15 months after Albert's death in a letter written on black-bordered mourning paper saying she 'can only hope never to live to old age but be allowed to rejoin her beloved and loyal husband before many years elapse'. Psychiatrists who have reviewed the queen's last journals believe she was suffering from a major depressive disorder.

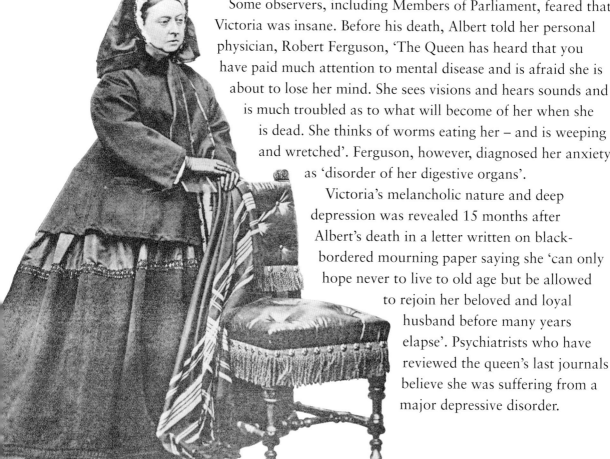

Below: Victoria's intense mourning after Albert's death also depressed her subjects and created a near crisis with Parliament.

TREATING DEPRESSION

Depression was normally called 'melancholy' in Victorian times. Doctors used the term for patients who avoided others and had a sorrowful nature, usually focusing on one subject that had caused their despair (as Victoria's grief after Albert's death). Without drugs for the condition, doctors treated depression by prescribing rest, a healthy diet and exercise in fresh air. More intense treatments included taking morphia (morphine) and drinking alcohol. One doctor advised having rum or sherry on arising, port with breakfast, two glasses of sherry at lunch, stout or port wine at dinner and stout or ale at bedtime along with morphia.

By 1870, the medical profession had established a link between thyroid deficiency and depression. Injections of animal thyroid extract were introduced and had some success.

Victorians with severe depression were considered suicidal. Poor patients were committed to an asylum, where their sense of isolation could increase and cause them to be diagnosed as insane. In the second half of the century, doctors used electrotherapy. The Sussex Asylum in 1873 gave electrical treatment 26 times to a female suicidal patient and reported that she appeared much brighter, conversed rationally and employed herself skilfully in needlework. She was judged cured and discharged.

Above: The Diamond Jubilee included a six-mile procession. The queen remained in the state coach because of her painful arthritis.

3

THE PEOPLE

Who lived through the Victorian era and what were they like? Society's customs and values obviously shaped their character, but how did people react as the nineteenth century progressed? The Victorians, it turns out, were not all meek followers.

THE FIRST image that might come to mind is of Victorian families leading decent lives based on hard work, strong religious beliefs and pride in the accomplishments of their society and country. This picture goes quickly out of focus when the vast majority, the poor, are considered.

The reality was that the Victorians' moral society had many immoral members according to its standards. Husbands beat wives and both sexes committed adultery, sometimes with their spouse's permission. Aristocrats seduced their helpless servants. The writer Oscar Wilde violated the law against homosexuality, as did many others.

At the same time, the better Victorian society remained at war against those who sinned. Even William Gladstone walked the dark streets of London before and while he was prime minister

Opposite: A young married Victorian couple in proper dress and serious mood pose for a typical formal portrait. Note that the man has a prosthetic right hand.

THE WILDE-v-QUEENSBERRY CASE
AND HOW IT ENDED

Mr OSCAR WILDE IN THE WITNESS BOX

Mr CARSON QC CROSS-EXAMINES WILDE

LORD A DOUGLAS

AT THE OLD BAILEY

ARREST OF WILDE AT THE CADOGAN HOTEL

PARKER GIVING EVIDENCE

TAYLOR JOINS WILDE IN THE DOCK

AT BOW STREET   IN THE POLICE CELL

Above: British newspapers followed Wilde's spectacular downfall every step of the way, as seen in this cartoon coverage.

intent on finding prostitutes, returning with them to their rooms and trying to talk them out of their godless lives, apparently without ever falling for their charms.

VICTORIAN SEX

A middle-class wife in the Victorian family was considered a domestic goddess who was submissive and kept the home as a refuge for her husband returning from the troubles of public life. She was considered to be incomplete without children. Sex was for procreation, not enjoyment. The gynaecological doctor William Acton wrote in 1857 that 'the majority of women (happily for them) are not very much troubled by sexual feelings of any kind'.

By the end of the century, however, Sigmund Freud and others would demonstrate that many women were repressed and frustrated. Their husbands, despite the generally accepted double standard, also suffered from their moral failures regarding sex, such as extramarital affairs or repressed homosexuality. Fears did exist, from the realistic danger of venereal diseases, especially syphilis, to the unrealistic worry about 'the solitary vice', masturbation, which was said to lead to insanity and even death.

Many superstitions existed concerning sexual unions. Guidebooks and manuals warned that having sex standing up would cause cancer; a child begat on stairs would probably be born with a crooked back; a man whose mind wandered during sex would produce 'inferior offspring'; an unfaithful husband would have unhappy children who would be 'weak and wretched', and any child conceived without true love would turn out to be 'ill-looking, sour and spiritless'.

Despite misinformation about sex in all classes, the reality was that many couples did enjoy sex together, and women were not as shy or frigid as some in society wished. Dour Queen Victoria herself was known to love sex. She wrote in her diary about her wedding night: 'It was a gratifying and bewildering experience. I never, never spent such an evening. His excessive love and affections gave me feelings of heavenly love and happiness. He clasped me in his arms and we kissed each other again and again.'

THE ADVENT OF SEXOLOGY
Richard von Krafft-Ebing (1840–1902), a German aristocrat, was a pioneering sexologist who shocked Victorians with his studies of female sexual pleasure, homosexuality, paedophilia, incest and necrophilia. He defined how sex should be studied by naming and classifying sexual aberrations, introducing the terms fetish, sadism, masochism and homosexuality. To discourage ordinary readers, he documented his 200 case studies in Latin in his groundbreaking 1886

GUIDEBOOKS WARNED THAT HAVING SEX STANDING UP WOULD CAUSE CANCER; A CHILD BEGAT ON STAIRS WOULD PROBABLY BE BORN WITH A CROOKED BACK.

Below: Richard von Krafft-Ebing dared to write about the unspoken sexual desires of Victorians and influenced Sigmund Freud's work.

work *Psychopathia Sexualis*, whose 12 editions influenced such psychologists as Sigmund Freud and Carl Jung. Krafft-Ebing also studied hypnosis, epilepsy and syphilis.

While studying at the University of Heidelberg, Krafft-Ebing developed an interest in the deviant sexuality of mental patients and criminals. He then taught psychiatry at several universities and worked in mental asylums. Krafft-Ebing believed sex

JAPAN'S SHUNGA ART

ISOLATED FROM THE PRUDISH ideals of Victorian Christians, the Japanese in the nineteenth century embraced sexual pleasure. This was displayed in their *shunga* art, depicting explicit sex without shame, including homosexual encounters. Women were depicted as equals enjoying sex. *Shunga* paintings were given to brides on their wedding night and as gifts. When one was presented to Commodore Matthew Perry, the American who visited Japan in 1853, his lieutenant noted it was 'proof of the lewdness of this exclusive people'. *Shunga* became a European favourite in the late Victorian period, praised by such artists as John Singer Sargent, Rodin and Toulouse-Lautrec.

Above: Shunga art was usually produced as woodblock prints. Many major Japanese artists produced erotic art without hurting their reputation.

was 'the most important factor in social existence'. Although he studied deviant sex, he held to romantic Victorian ideas, saying 'Christianity raised the union of the sexes to a sublime position of making woman socially the equal of man and by elevating the bond of love to a moral and religious institution'. Despite the equality of the sexes, he said women had little or no sexual desire if they were 'physically and mentally normal and properly educated'.

Above: Women's rights in divorce cases improved during the nineteenth century, but court cases remained biased in favour of the husband.

DIVORCE AND ADULTERY

In the early Victorian era, a married woman had virtually no rights. Her property became her husband's, as did their children and even herself. He could beat her and lock her up, knowing the authorities avoided interference in marital relations. If she ran away for any time, he could even lock her out of their home.

ISABELLA ROBINSON

IN ONE OF THE most sensational divorce trials of the era, Henry Robinson, an engineer, attempted to divorce his wife, Isabella, after reading her diary when she was ill. He told of his 'horror and astonishment' on seeing details of her affair with a younger man, Dr Edward Lane. One florid entry read, 'I leaned back at last in silent joy in those arms I had so often dreamed of, and kissed the curls and smooth face, so radiant with beauty that had dazzled my outward and inward vision since I first saw him'.

Despite Henry's own open adultery, which had produced two children, he threw his wife out, took custody of their two children and sued to end their 12-year marriage. During the trial in 1865, female spectators were banned for fear of corrupting their morals. Isabella claimed her diary entries were fiction and written because she had been 'labouring under sexual hallucinations' caused by a 'disease of the womb'. The jury was sympathetic to her defence of falling under a 'species of insanity' and denied the divorce. This result also saved the reputation of 27-year-old Dr Lane, who denied any wrongdoing, as well as his marriage and medical practice.

Britain's Matrimonial Causes Act of 1857, commonly called the Divorce Act, made divorce officially legal. Prior to its passage, divorce was a long and expensive process that had to be approved by the Church of England followed by a Private Act of Parliament that cost about £1000 even if uncontested. Britain was the only Protestant European country not providing a civil divorce. This was changed by setting up the Court for Divorce and Matrimonial Causes, which soon became crowded with middle-class cases.

Adultery remained the only reason for divorce. The new act allowed a man to divorce his wife for adultery, but a woman could only divorce if adultery was accompanied by 'life-threatening cruelty', bigamy, incest, rape, sodomy, bestiality or desertion for two years or more. Women did make gains, however, as wives could now allege cruelty and desertion along with adultery. The act also protected divorced, separated and deserted wives. While it was being written, Queen Victoria gave instructions that scandalous stories should not be included, saying 'none of the French novels from which careful parents try to protect their children can be as bad as what is daily brought and laid upon the breakfast table of every educated family in England'.

CATHERINE 'SKITTLES' WALTERS

Known as the last renowned courtesan, Catherine Walters (1839–1920) was a native of Liverpool and settled in London, where she gained her nickname 'Skittles' by working in a skittle (bowling) alley. Her beauty and discretion destined her for finer

STAGED ADULTERY

BRITAIN'S STRICT divorce laws were a nuisance to couples who agreed their marriages were not working. Adultery was the only allowed reason for divorce. If this sin had not happened, couples sometimes worked together to fake the act. One spouse, normally the husband, would sacrifice his good name for their freedom. The staged event involved hiring a woman to portray the 'mistress' and waiting together in bed with her partially dressed for his wife to burst in with her fake detective and photographer. To maintain dignity, the man might be dressed and wearing a top hat. Even if authorities were certain a staged adultery had taken place, judges had no witnesses to convict. Eventually such cases were thrown out as collusive shams.

things. She early attracted admirers as an accomplished horsewoman, as crowds gathered to watch her ride in Hyde Park's Rotten Row wearing an elegant silk hat and veil, one of the displays that made her a trendsetter.

Victorian women were shocked and envious. Among Catherine's numerous lovers and benefactors were aristocrats, politicians, intellectuals and royals. They included the Prince of Wales (later Edward VII) and Napoleon III. She twice went with lovers to America during the Civil War: with the aristocrat Aubrey de Vere Beauclerk and with Spencer Cavendish, Marquess of Hartington (known as 'Harty Tarty'), who became the Duke of Devonshire. The poet Wilfred Scawen Blunt became so infatuated with Catherine that he wrote about her for years, even though they had spent only a few hours together.

Catherine accumulated wealth and lived in grand style in Mayfair while owning other houses in Britain and France. She retired around 1890 and died in 1920 at the age of 81.

Left: The Prince of Wales sent over 300 letters to Catherine Walters. When he asked for them back, she graciously returned them.

PROSTITUTION

Prostitution had a wider meaning to Victorians. Besides streetwalkers, the term could refer to loose women who engaged in sex for pleasure, those with illegitimate children, and even women who lived with men unmarried. The greatest concern by far was 'the Great Social Evil' – the legions of women soliciting on city streets, holding up their skirts to encourage business. Their estimated numbers in London varied greatly. Police records in 1868 counted 6515, while other unofficial estimates ranged from 80,000 to 219,000. Some worked in brothels or their own neighbourhoods, but many preferred such notorious areas as the dockyards and streets near Waterloo Station, where they displayed themselves virtually naked in windows. Unfortunate victims of such free access to sex were respectable women who were harassed and accosted in public, especially when wearing eye-catching clothes.

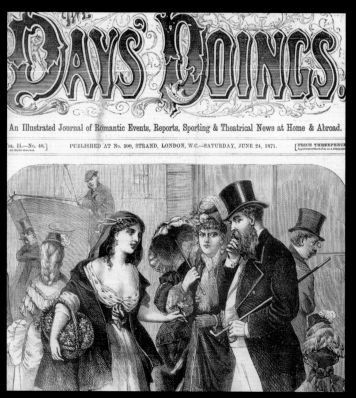

An Illustrated Journal of Romantic Events, Reports, Sporting & Theatrical News at Home & Abroad.

Above: It was an awkward but not rare occasion in London when a wife realized a street girl knew her husband.

Child prostitutes were often seen on the streets. In 1848, hospitals treated nearly 2700 girls between the ages of 11 and 16 for venereal diseases, primarily the result of prostitution. This was a prime reason in 1875 that the age of consent was raised from 12 to 13 years. It had little effect, and a Parliamentary committee in 1881 reported that child prostitution was out of control. Four years later, 16 became the new age of consent.

Venereal diseases became rampant by the middle of the century, and Parliament passed three Contagious Disease Acts in 1864, 1866 and 1869. The idea was to protect members of the military. The 1869 act forced prostitutes to be examined periodically and to be held in hospitals for a year if necessary. They were also prohibited from soliciting within 15 miles (24km) of military bases and seaports. Surprisingly, a campaign against the acts involved women's groups, who felt they legalized prostitution and also humiliated those forced on the streets by poverty.

ITALY'S FIRST VICE LAW

As industrialization expanded in Italy, rural women moved in large numbers to the cities, where poverty turned many to prostitution. Respectable families regarded streetwalkers as promiscuous sexual deviants and part of the idle poor. Their growing numbers created much fear because of their links to criminals. The government, however, regarded prostitution as a necessary social evil. One of the first laws after Italian unification in 1861 was the *Regolamentazione*, passed that year to legalize and control the profession. A moral police was created to survey prostitutes who would then be registered, examined and treated. Also known as the Cavour Regulation after Italy's first prime minister, Camillo Benso di Cavour, it was modelled on similar laws in France and Belgium.

Among the restrictions were unannounced police inspections of brothels, which were banned from operating games, serving food or drink and conducting entertainments such as music, dancing and parties. A brothel's windows had to be shuttered and became

JOSEPHINE BUTLER

Above: Josephine Butler campaigned against the trafficking of women and children, exposing such a trade from Belgium to Britain.

AN AVID FEMINIST, Josephine Butler (1828–1906) was a Northumberland aristocrat who despaired about the hopeless condition of prostitutes. She often ventured into the docks and streets of Liverpool to locate girls forced into the sex trade. Her biggest success was campaigning to have the Contagious Diseases Act repealed, being particularly angry at genital examinations to determine sexual infections in girls as young as 13. Not everyone agreed. When she made speeches against the 'steel rape' or 'instrumental rape' of young girls by 'terrible aristocratic doctors', crowds often pelted her with rotten fruit. In 1886, however, Josephine sat in the Commons' public gallery to watch the act being repealed.

known popularly as a 'closed house'. Some rights were given to prostitutes. Madams were not allowed to mistreat them, and 'individual prostitutes' could operate legally in private homes and were given hospital care, especially to prevent and treat venereal diseases.

Right: Italian prostitutes were criminal types using feminine cunning to avoid jail, wrote the Italian criminologist Caesar Lombroso in 1876.

LULU WHITE

Born in Alabama in 1868, Lulu White was a model for pornographic photos in the 1880s before opening Mahogany Hall, an elite brothel in New Orleans, in 1894. Located in Storyville, the red-light district designated as such by municipal ordinance, her four-storey marble brothel claimed to be the most elegant in New Orleans, featuring five parlours 'handsomely furnished' with mirrored walls and ceilings and 15 bedrooms. She promoted her prostitutes as all being exotic 'octoroons' (one-eighth black). Her white-only clients included some of the most prominent and wealthy men in Louisiana. As a jazz pianist played, prostitutes performed their 'naked dance' while clients sipped champagne. Lulu became one of the city's most successful madams and claimed to own the largest jewel collection in the South, dubbing herself the 'Diamond Queen'. Her establishment has been immortalized in the jazz song 'Mahogany Stomp', recorded by Louis Armstrong and others.

Lulu White's later years were not so enjoyable. After opening a brothel too close to a military base in 1918, she served three months of a year's sentence in prison before President Woodrow Wilson pardoned her because of poor health. She recovered and operated another brothel in New Orleans until her death in 1931.

Above: Lulu White's promotional booklet bragged about her jewels, saying they were like 'the lights of the St. Louis Exposition'.

MAGDALENE ASYLUMS

Ireland's Magdalene institutions, also known as Magdalene Laundries, were workhouses for 'fallen' women originally established in 1765 to reform prostitutes. They were run by Roman Catholic nuns. Some 30,000 women and girls were sent there by their families, priests and the state until the final one closed in 1996. Most of the inmates, called 'Maggies' by others, were held against their will and remained there until death,

DURING THE VICTORIAN YEARS, THE ASYLUMS HOUSED UNWED MOTHERS, PROSTITUTES AND EVEN WOMEN AND GIRLS SENT AS A PREVENTATIVE MEASURE...

working as virtually slave labourers. Escapes were attempted but usually failed, with the public often assisting their capture. Magdalene asylums also existed in Scotland and other countries.

During the Victorian years, the asylums housed unwed mothers, prostitutes and even women and girls sent as a preventative measure, because their promiscuous behaviour was deemed a danger to themselves and others. Usually known as penitents, each was given a new name, kept in solitary confinement for the first three months, had her hair cut short and assigned hard labour without pay to atone for her sins. If she had children, they were housed in an orphanage and could not contact their mother.

The brutal treatment of the fallen women was unknown until 1993, when a mass grave of 155 bodies was discovered in the grounds of a Dublin asylum. Following this, numerous former inmates revealed the physical, sexual and psychological abuse they had endured. The Irish government offered an apology along with £30 million in compensation to victims still living.

Below: Babies of unwed mothers in Magdalene Laundries are still being found. Some 800 were discovered in County Galway, Ireland, in 2017.

CHINA'S FIRST MENTAL HOSPITAL

The mentally ill in China in the nineteenth century were normally confined to dark rooms by their families. If they left the house, people would point them out and laugh, even throwing stones at them. They were kept so isolated that mental disease was not considered a major problem. One American who changed this was Dr John Kerr, who ran the Ophthalmic Hospital in Canton (now Guangzhou) from 1854 for more than 40 years, treating nearly one million patients. One of his medical students was Sun Yat-Sen, the first president of China.

Kerr won the support of Professor Edward Thwing of the American Presbyterian Mission, who delivered a talk in 1890 on 'Western methods with Insane Chinese'. The two of them appealed to wealthy residents in Hong Kong and Canton to help fund a mental hospital, but the locals had no interest in outsiders telling them what was needed.

Kerr pushed on and in 1891 optimistically bought three acres in Canton. A former medical missionary then surprised him by donating money for the building. In 1897, the 24-room Refuge for the Insane, China's first mental hospital, was completed. The following year, the first patient arrived, unable to walk and still bound in the chains that had kept him attached to a stone for three years. The second patient was a woman found with a chain around her neck attached to the floor.

Kerr introduced humane treatment unknown in the country. He avoided force and restraint, explaining that his patients were ill and would be given rest and recreation, as well as gainful employment if possible. The local Chinese authorities were delighted to be relieved of the burden of caring for these people, and were amazed at Kerr's results – so much so they paid an annual allowance for patient care. The Refuge for the Insane expanded to 500 beds and continued with more success until closing in 1937. Today's modern Guangzhou Huiai Hospital is an outgrowth of Kerr's institution.

Above: Sun Yat-Sen became John Kerr's medical student in 1886 and convinced him to stop separating male and female students.

Right: Simeon Solomon (pictured) was a close friend of the Victorian poet Algernon Charles Swinburne, who abruptly dropped him after his arrest.

HOMOSEXUALITY

The subject of homosexuality was not openly discussed in Victorian society, because no words existed to describe the concept. Although it was a hanging offence in Britain until 1861, Victorians were surprisingly tolerant of acts done in privacy. Those in public places, however, were seldom ignored by the police. Many death sentences for men arrested in the mid-nineteenth century were automatically converted to transportation.

PRIVATE MALE HOMOSEXUAL ACTS BEHIND CLOSED DOORS WERE NOT MADE A CRIMINAL OFFENCE UNTIL 1885.

A more relaxed attitude was soon evident. In 1873, the fashionable pre-Raphaelite artist Simeon Solomon, 33, known for painting handsome boys, was caught having sex with an illiterate stableman in a London public lavatory. They were arrested for the 'abominable crime of buggery'. The worker, 60, was given 18 months of hard labour, while Solomon received a fine of £100. The next year he was arrested in a Paris public urinal with a male prostitute and spent three months in jail. He

Private male homosexual acts behind closed doors were not made a criminal offence until 1885. The playwright Oscar Wilde became the act's first victim in 1895, but only after he had sued his partner's father for calling him a homosexual. Lesbianism was to have been included in the legislation, but was omitted after Queen Victoria declared such a thing was impossible.

Below: Simeon Solomon's 1864 painting 'Sappho and Erinna in the Garden Mytelene' depicts their lesbian relationship on the island of Lesbos.

JACK SAUL

ALSO KNOWN AS DUBLIN Jack, Saul was a poor Irish Catholic working as a popular rent boy in a secret male brothel at 19 Cleveland Street in London. Jack wrote an infamous 1881 anonymous pornographic memoir, *The Sins of the Cities of the Plain*, describing his life as a 'Mary Ann', a male prostitute dressing as a woman. The establishment also kept several young telegraph boys whose sexual services were rented by aristocrats. A scandal broke on 4 July 1889 when one admitted this to police, saying he was paid four shillings for each act. By the next year, about 60 clients had been identified, and 22 had fled the country, including the owner Charles Hammond. One rumoured client was Prince Albert Victor, Queen Victoria's grandson and second in line to the throne. The rent boys were convicted of gross indecency and given sentences of four to nine months with hard labour.

In 1890, Saul, then in his early 30s, became a witness in a libel court case brought by the Earl of Euston against a newspaper that had reported he was a patron of the brothel. During his testimony, Dublin Jack's lewd language and descriptions of sex acts shocked the court. The earl won his case even though Jack described various acts the two of them had done. Despite his testimony being incriminating, Jack was not prosecuted. He eventually returned to Dublin to work as a butler and died at the age of 46.

Above: Prince Albert Victor was strongly rumoured to have visited the male brothel, but was never named by Jack Saul.

OSCAR WILDE

The brilliant playwright and wit Oscar Wilde (1854–1900) appeared to have the perfect family, married with two sons. At the same time, he carried on a homosexual relationship with Lord Alfred Douglas and began to flout it openly. By 1895, he was at the peak of his career, as his comedy *The Importance of Being Earnest* became a great success in London. That same year, however, he made a crucial mistake. The Marquess of Queensberry, Douglas' father, accused him in a note of being a 'somdomite' (misspelling the word 'sodomite'). Rather than ignoring this, Wilde sued for criminal libel at the urging of Douglas. When the testimony at the trial began to favour the marquess, Wilde dropped the suit. Friends urged him to flee to France, but he believed his fame would keep him safe. However, he was arrested for gross indecency with men, the first person to be prosecuted under the 1885 homosexual law.

Above: Oscar Wilde (left) posed with his lover, Lord Alfred Douglas. Wilde's biggest mistake was to sue Douglas' father.

The first trial resulted in a hung jury but a second one convicted him. Wilde was sentenced to two years in Reading Gaol with hard labour, having to pick coarse rope apart until his hands bled and also walk on a treadmill each day. While there, he wrote to Douglas accusing him of encouraging his homosexuality and distracting him from work. When freed in 1897, Wilde was a mental and physical wreck, as well as being bankrupt. After spending time in France and Italy and writing *The Ballad of Reading Gaol* in 1898, he settled in a flat in Paris and hosted a few remaining friends before dying in 1900.

DR JAMES BARRY

For all the fame James Barry (1789–1865) earned as a leading British military surgeon and inspector of military hospitals, his name became infamous at his death when it was discovered 'he'

Above: Margaret Ann
Buckley, shown with her
servant John, became the
first woman to practise
medicine in Britain.

was a woman. Barry had deceived Edinburgh
University, the Royal College of Surgeons
and the British Army to become the UK's first
woman doctor.

Born Margaret Ann Buckley in Cork,
Ireland, she disguised herself as a boy and
assumed the name of her rich uncle, the
celebrated artist James Barry, who helped her
enrol in Edinburgh. She obtained her medical
degree in 1812 and the next year joined
the army as an assistant surgeon. Margaret
served in Cape Town, South Africa, where
she began her lifelong campaign to reorganize
health care emphasizing hygiene. She
travelled the world from the Mediterranean
to Canada, assuming a rough masculine
attitude, telling off Florence Nightingale at
one point, and even fighting a duel with a
fellow officer. Margaret performed one of the first successful
caesareans and in 1848 wrote a definitive report on cholera.

When she died of dysentery in 1865, Margaret's secret life
as James Barry was uncovered by the woman who laid out and
washed the body, describing her as 'a perfect woman'. Several
people who knew her claimed they always knew the doctor
was female. Others speculated that Barry was a hermaphrodite,
having characteristics of both sexes. Asked whether Barry was
male or female, the doctor who signed the death certificate
declared 'it's none of my business'.

A FEMALE CIVIL WAR SOLDIER

Opposite: After the Civil
War, Sarah Edmondson
married in Canada
and had three children.
Returning to the US, they
adopted two boys.

Both sides in the American Civil War had women soldiers who
fought disguised as men. They cut their hair short, bound their
breasts, wore layered or loose uniforms and smeared their faces
with dirt. Their motivations were usually patriotism, adventure
or escape from their former lives. Of an estimated 400 who did
this, one of the best-documented cases was Sarah Emma Evelyn
Edmondson (1841–1898).

IT WAS ONLY IN THE NINETEENTH CENTURY THAT A TRUE MIDDLE CLASS EMERGED TO USE THEIR NEW MONEY TO CONTEST THE RULE OF OLD MONEY.

Born in New Brunswick, Canada, Sarah moved to the United States to escape an arranged marriage and assumed a man's dress and name, Franklin Thompson. When the war began in 1861, she enlisted as Thompson, a private. At first she was a nurse and mail carrier, then assumed several disguises to gather intelligence behind enemy lines, going as a black male slave and as a female Irish peddler. Sarah fought in several engagements. When her horse was killed at the Second Battle of Bull Run in August 1862, she switched to a mule and fell off, suffering a broken leg and internal injuries.

The following year, she contracted malaria and, fearing discovery by doctors, left without leave. Recovering, she attempted to return to duty only to learn that Franklin Thompson had been charged with desertion. Sarah therefore dropped the hoax and served the remainder of the war as a nurse in Washington, DC. She published her memoirs in 1864 to great success and gave the profits to the US War Relief Fund. Since she had admitted her military deception, Sarah was given an honourable discharge and an army pension. In 1897, she was the only woman admitted as a member of the Grand Army of the Republic.

THE CLASS SYSTEM

Britain's ancient and engrained social class system was led by the aristocracy, who were well separated from the mass of labourers and artisans. Many small businesses existed, but it was only in the nineteenth century that a true middle class emerged to use their new money to contest the rule of old money. Those in the upwardly mobile middle class could now aspire to be gentlemen and ladies through education and morality.

The **upper class,** in particular the nobility, retained their social, political and military leadership throughout the Victorian years. This involved the rights of heredity, a family seat and enough income to avoid any unpleasant type of work. This old aristocracy, however, was being blended into a new upper class based on commerce, industry and the professions.

Members of the **middle class** were well off and careful to maintain proper manners and values. The Victorians coined the term 'bourgeoisie' for this respectable class of businessmen and professionals. The narrow conventions they lived under, however, produced new stress for men and boredom for women.

The **lower middle class** were the 'shabby genteel' Victorians who imitated the middle class if possible by living a respectable life, having a servant and keeping their wives and daughters away from everyday jobs.

The **working class**, skilled and unskilled, was still at the bottom, although many strived to move up the social ladder. This was difficult because labourers had little chance for an advanced or higher education, remaining uneducated and doomed to poverty. Research done in London and York in 1898 found that a third of this class were faced with starvation.

Below: This 1843 depiction of the class system, 'Capital and Labour', reflects the Victorians' uneasiness over their exploitative social divisions.

ARISTOCRATIC ABUSE

THE POWERS OF VICTORIAN aristocrats were felt from Parliament to the estates and villages they controlled. A darker side of their authority was often felt within their impressive houses, where servant girls of the lower classes, who spent years close to their wealthy employers, were regarded as virtually their property and taken at their pleasure. Sometimes the victims were willing in hopes of favours from their masters, but many times they were raped without recourse and perhaps left with an illegitimate, albeit blue-blooded, child. Pregnancy usually meant dismissal without complaint, since servants required a reference for their next employment.

THE TICHBORNE CLAIMANT

Sir Roger Tichborne was a British aristocrat who at the age of 24 sailed off on a South American adventure. After working in the region, in 1854 he boarded a ship named the *Bella* on the way to the West Indies. Along the way it sunk, and Tichborne was declared dead the following year. His mother, Lady Henriette, held out hope and advertised in international newspapers that her missing son was heir of all the family estates. She also offered a 'most liberal reward' for information about his fate.

PREGNANCY USUALLY MEANT DISMISSAL WITHOUT COMPLAINT, SINCE SERVANTS REQUIRED A REFERENCE FOR THEIR NEXT EMPLOYMENT.

Reading this, a butcher in Wagga Wagga, New South Wales, Australia, calling himself Tom Castro, was more interested in the inheritance than the reward. He had a solicitor write to Lady Henriette in 1865 claiming he was her lost son. Lady Henriette was overjoyed and sent for Castro. Although his appearance had changed, it had been 10 years, and she embraced him as her son and granted him an allowance of £1000 a year. The family were more suspicious, as Castro could not speak French, his original language; he had been born in Paris and spent his youth there. The family made inquiries in Australia and discovered that Tom Castro was actually Arthur Orton, a Londoner.

Lady Henriette died in 1868, but Orton had had enough time to research Sir Roger and continued his sham. The family took him to court in a civil trial that fascinated the newspapers and public. More than 100 defence witnesses supported Orton's claim, but the prosecution made telling points, such as his missing tattoos and lack of French language. After a second criminal trial, he was sentenced to 14 years of hard labour. The two trials had taken nearly a year, then a British record. He served 10 years, being released in 1884 after a campaign by many, including George Bernard Shaw, who believed the aristocracy was mistreating a working-class person.

Orton confessed 11 years later that he was an imposter in order to receive a payment from a newspaper for his story.

Above: Starting at his Australian butcher's shop, Arthur Orton made a transition from the boorish Tom Castro to aristocratic Roger Tichborne.

Crown Solicitor   Mr. C. Barber Mr. Hawkins, Q.C. Mr. Fredk. Bowker Mr. Bowen   Mr. Serjeant Parry Tichborne Bondholder   Treasury Solicitor's Chief Clerk   Mr. McMahon   Dr. Kenealy   The Defendant   Andrew Bogle, Jun. Mr. G. H. Wholley, M.P.

THE TICHBORNE CASE—"PRO AND CON"
(A SKETCH OF THE COURT FROM THE "WELL" DURING DR. KENEALY'S SPEECH)

Above: The main protagonists were sketched during the famous Tichborne Claimant case of 1871 that ended with his conviction of perjury.

He then retracted the confession and used the money to open a tobacconist's shop in Islington that failed. He died in 1898 and was officially recognized as Tichborne on his death certificate and a plate on his coffin. He was buried in an unmarked pauper's grave with some 5000 people attending the funeral.

A DUKE'S DOUBLE LIFE
The Fifth Duke of Portland was a rich, eccentric man close to being deranged. He ate one chicken each day alone in one room of his vast Welbeck Abbey in Nottinghamshire, and avoided contact with anybody. He instructed servants to look away as he passed by, even in his large garden. If he became ill, the doctor was called but could not see him. The duke shouted his symptoms through a door, and the doctor shouted back his

diagnosis and instructions. If he had to go out in public, he was covered by three overcoats, a top hat and an umbrella, and his carriage windows were blocked by curtains. Most locals therefore had no idea what he looked like.

This made it easy for him to assume another identity. Who would have thought the reclusive Thomas Druce, who owned a London shop, was actually a duke? Both had the same height, build and appearance. Druce used a curtain to shield his office from staff and told them to ignore him when he came out. Druce would disappear from his Baker Street Bazaar when the duke was at Welbeck Abbey and return when the duke left his estate. All this came to an end in 1864 when a funeral and burial were held for Druce, just as the duke returned home to begin a massive building project. Thousands of workers were employed to construct a ballroom for 2000 guests, a riding school, a billiard room, a library and other rooms, all underground, all connected by miles of tunnels and all used only by the duke, who died in 1879.

In 1896, a woman on Baker Street, Anna Maria Druce, requested that her father-in-law's coffin be dug up and opened to prove that the funeral of Druce (the duke) had been faked. This was to prove her son the rightful Sixth Duke of Portland able to inherit the fortune. Newspapers leapt to her cause, but her case went nowhere and in 1903 she ended up in an insane asylum. Her family continued to press the claim, and in 1906 an underground passage was discovered between the shop and Druce's house, suggesting another tunnel for the duke. The next year, the coffin was opened and found to contain a body, so the case was dismissed as 'frivolous and vexatious', but many still believed the men's similarities proved they were one and the same.

Below: Many remained convinced that Thomas Druce was actually William John Cavendish-Scott-Bentinck, the Fifth Duke of Portland.

POLICE
THE ILLUSTRATED
NEWS
LAW COURTS AND WEEKLY RECORD

SISTER OF VICTIM

FIFTH VICTIM

MORTUARY

THE BERNER ST. VICTIM.

INSPECTOR REID

INQUEST ON FIFTH VICTIM AT ST. GEORES INT EA

TWO MORE WHITECHAPEL HORRORS. WHEN WILL THE MURDERER BE CAPTURED

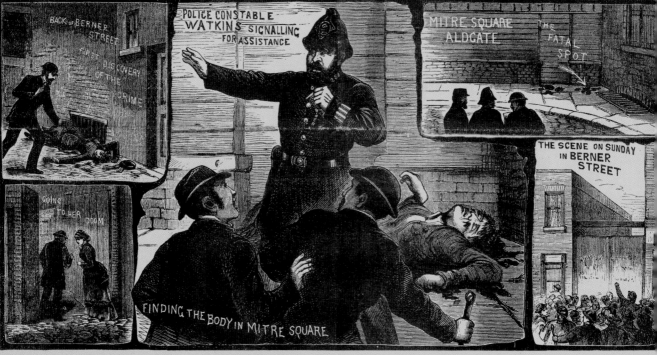

BACK OF BERNER STREET

FIRST DISCOVERY OF THE CRIME

POLICE CONSTABLE WATKINS SIGNALLING FOR ASSISTANCE

MITRE SQUARE ALDGATE

THE FATAL SPOT

GOING TO HER DOOM

FINDING THE BODY IN MITRE SQUARE

THE SCENE ON SUNDAY IN BERNER STREET

EXTERIOR OF THE GATE

4

CRIME AND PUNISHMENT

Victorian cities were breeding grounds for violence and crime. The prime reasons included the many crowded neighbourhoods of the poor and an ebb and flow of strangers who were displaced by the Industrial Revolution.

Most violent attacks in London happened in its East End, but even exclusive areas suffered minor crimes such as pickpocketing in the daytime and physical attacks after dark. The fear this caused was turned into near panic by newspapers using overblown headlines to emphasize danger on the streets. Murder stories reached a frenzy with Jack the Ripper, the vicious serial killer, in 1888. He was never identified, prolonging the terror. Equally brutal murders occurred throughout the Victorian era, including those by Amelia Dyer, who became Britain's worst ever serial killer, responsible for the deaths of some 400 children. Police investigations were often slow, depending on basic observation, but technology came to the rescue in later years. The telegraph was used between London and Chicago to help bring 'the Lambeth Poisoner' to justice in 1892.

Opposite: Sensational newspapers spread fear of Jack the Ripper. This article recounts the murders of Elizabeth Stride and Catharine Eddowes.

Non-violent crime was widespread, from petty thievery to monumental fraud. An American gang robbed the Bank of England of £100,000 in the Great Fraud of 1873 and were apprehended in Edinburgh, New York and Havana, resulting in two life sentences. Almost everyone arrested in Victorian years went to jail, including pickpockets and those who stole a loaf of bread. London's growing prison population led to many convicts being transported to Australia and others housed in large prison hulks docked on the Thames.

POCKETS TO PICK

In his 1838 novel *Oliver Twist*, Charles Dickens created a ring of child pickpockets run by the lovable rogue Fagin. The Artful Dodger was fictional but easily recognized by Dickens' readers. Victorian London's overcrowded streets were ripe for picking, overrun by ragged urchins, some as young as five, out to steal purses, handkerchiefs and anything else that was loose. Known

Above: Any distraction on London's streets created an opportunity for child pickpockets who were drawn to the excitement of gang life.

THE ORANGE BOY

ONE LONDON PICKPOCKET, 11, was known as 'the orange boy'. He beseeched passers-by to 'buy a few oranges of a poor orphan who hadn't a bit of bread to eat'. While talking, he pushed his basket against his victims, who later realized their purse was gone. One reader penned a letter to

The Times on 5 March 1850 warning: 'Ladies, young and old, never carry your purses in your pockets; beware of canting beggars, and beggars of all sorts, that infest the streets; and, above all, keep a watchful eye about you and give the widest possible berth to THE ORANGE BOY'.

as natty lads, the boys were quick at distraction and had quick fingers. Some preferred to work alone, but more success came from roaming in packs.

Among the criminal bosses who trained youths in 1855 was Charles King. His gang of professional pickpockets included John Reeves, 13, who once stole £100 in one week. Any commotion on the streets was good picking time. Martin Gavin, 11, was tried in 1840 for lifting a gentleman's handkerchief in a crowd that gathered around an accident. At one time, 5000 handkerchiefs a week were stolen to be hung outside shops where the victims could go to buy back their property.

Skilled pickpockets believed they would never be apprehended, but this was a bad bet: anybody caught could be executed, though for children this was almost always commuted to a lesser sentence, such as prison or transportation. Between 1830 and 1860, more than half of the pickpockets tried at London's Old Bailey were younger than 20.

TRANSPORTATION

The Victorians continued a system begun in 1717 to ship criminals overseas. Transportation solved several problems: jails were less crowded, many types of undesirables were removed from Britain forever, and necessary labour was provided for the expanding colonies. Those shipped off ranged from children stealing bread to hardened criminals who had their death sentences commuted.

America had received the convicts until its War of Independence in 1776, when new penal colonies were set up in Australia and New Zealand. The

Below: Convicted female prisoners are depicted being sent to the French penal colony in New Caledonia, Australia.

MARY WADE

WHEN SHE DIED IN 1859 in Australia at the age of 82, Mary Wade was famous as the youngest convict ever transported there. As a child she swept London streets and begged. When 12, she was sentenced in 1789 to death by hanging for stealing a frock from an 8-year-old girl. Commuted, Mary was transported on an 11-month voyage. She had several children and married Jonathan Brooker, settling in the Illawarra region of New South Wales. He died in 1833, 26 years before her.

Mary lived to see more than 300 of her descendants. Australia's former Prime Minister Kevin Rudd is among tens of thousands living today.

List of Convicts embarked on board the Merchantman 27th June from Portland, for removal to Western Australia

first convict fleet arrived in 1788 at Botany Bay in Australia. The colony of New South Wales was officially the penal colony, and by the mid-1800s several other destinations were used. About 20 per cent of those transported were women, who were sent to work in 'female factories'.

Included among the guilty were political prisoners such as Irish nationalists. By 1852, some 1800 were from Wales; many spoke only Welsh, which isolated them even more. All convicts could expect to be assigned to hard labour, usually working on roads, quarries and farms. Their new sentences generally ran from seven to 14 years, but they could be released for good behaviour by a ticket of leave, certificate of freedom, conditional pardon or absolute pardon. Prisoners could even return to Britain if given the latter.

Public opinion in both countries led to transportation ending in 1868. Australians had seen too many criminals settling on their land, and the British saw little drop in the crime rate as convicts were given a free journey to a new life. During its 80-year history, transportation had sent about 162,000 prisoners to Australia on 806 ships. About 70 per cent had come from England and Wales, 24 per cent from Ireland and five per cent from Scotland. Other criminals also arrived in Australia from Canada, India and China.

A PROPHET'S MURDER

In 1823, Joseph Smith said that an angel named Moroni told him of an ancient record about God's dealings with Native Americans.

Above: A Certificate of Freedom was granted to convicts in an Australia penal colony when they had served their sentence.

Smith announced he had found this record in 1827 on thin golden plates, and God gave him the power to translate *The Book of Mormon*. Three years later, he founded the Church of Jesus Christ of Latter-Day Saints, becoming its first president. He plunged into his life's work in Ohio, Missouri and Illinois, where he established Mormon temples, founded towns, wrote volumes of scripture and sent missionaries to other countries. He even ran for president of the United States in 1844.

Controversy and persecution followed Smith everywhere. He wed as many as 40 wives; some were already married, and one was only 14 years old. This was one of the charges made by dissenting Mormons in Nauvoo, Illinois, who printed a newspaper to expose the 'abominations and whoredoms' of Smith and other church officials. When he ordered the paper closed, a riot pursued, and Smith and his brother Hyrum were imprisoned in Carthage, the county seat. He said, 'I am going like a lamb to the slaughter, but I am as calm as a summer's morning'. This was the chance many were waiting for; an angry mob of men with blackened faces stormed the jail on 27 June 1844 and shot both of them dead.

Opposite: Convicts' names were listed when embarking on the ship *Merchantman* from Portland, UK, to Western Australia on 1 July 1864.

Above: When Joseph Smith was murdered by a mob, the leadership of the Mormon church fell to Brigham Young.

The *Warsaw Signal* newspaper said the killings were a regrettable but justified response to the threat Smith posed to liberty. Five men were tried for the murders but all were acquitted. Two years later, Smith's successor Brigham Young led the Mormon community from Nauvoo, trekking west to settle in 1847 in Utah. Here they founded Salt Lake City as the home of their church, which now has some 16 million members worldwide.

MADELEINE SMITH

One of Scotland's most sensational trials involved a socialite, Madeleine Hamilton Smith, charged with the arsenic murder of her former lover, Pierre Emile L'Angelier. They had conducted a passionate affair, swapping secret letters pretending they were married. He wrote to 'Wifie mine' and she called herself his 'darling wife'.

Despite all this love, Madeleine became engaged to William Minnoch, a wealthy member of high society. She asked L'Angelier to return her letters, and added, 'I trust your honour as a gentleman that you will not reveal anything that may have passed between us'. He refused and threatened to show them to Minnoch and Madeleine's father, a well-known Glasgow architect. She agreed to spend more nights with him, but on two occasions during her visits L'Angelier became ill after she served him coffee. He informed friends that she probably poisoned him. He died in March 1857 and a post-mortem revealed a large amount of arsenic in his body. When police then discovered the letters, they arrested Madeleine.

A report of her scandalous trial said that Madeleine, 22, entered the dock with 'the air of a belle entering a ballroom or a box at the opera. Her steps were buoyant and she carried a silver-topped bottle of smelling salts. She was stylishly dressed and wore a pair of lavender gloves'. While in prison, she said she received hundreds of letters 'all from gentlemen offering consolation, their hearts and money'.

The prosecution based their case on motive and Madeleine's recent purchase of three doses of morphine. She said it was used to kill vermin and also diluted as a cosmetic. She claimed she had not seen L'Angelier for three weeks before he died, and her defence suggested he might have ended his own life. The jury took only half an hour to declare that murder was 'not proven', and she was set free. Soon after, she moved to London and married the Pre-Raphaelite painter George Wardle. After they divorced, she emigrated to the United States and wed again, dying at the age of 93 in 1927.

ONE OF SCOTLAND'S MOST SENSATIONAL TRIALS INVOLVED A SOCIALITE CHARGED WITH THE ARSENIC MURDER OF HER FORMER LOVER.

Below: The jury's verdict of 'not proven' did not mean 'not guilty' but that the evidence against Madeleine Smith was weak.

CONSTANCE CONFESSED TO A PRIEST THAT SHE HAD TAKEN THE CHILD TO THE PRIVY AND KILLED HIM WITH HER FATHER'S RAZOR.

THE ROAD HILL HOUSE MURDER

The murder of a three-year-old boy in an English country house on 29 June 1860 became Britain's first real detective story, as the public followed the investigation by Scotland Yard Detective Jonathan Jack Whicher. Some turned against him for revealing the corruption within the household, including sexual sins, jealousy, wayward children and disloyal servants. Most were variously considered as either suspects or victims.

Samuel and Mary Kent, a successful couple in Road, Wiltshire, had awakened to find their son Francis Saville missing from his cot. His body was discovered stuffed into the privy outside, with his neck slashed deeply. Local police suspected that the nursemaid Elizabeth Gough and her lover had killed the boy for disturbing them. Another prime suspect was Constance's brother, William. The investigation went nowhere, and Detective Whicher took over the case. He determined that Constance Emily Kent, 16, Saville's sullen half-sister, was guilty. When he arrested her on 16 July, however, the public was scornful of a working-class detective accusing such a lady of murder, and Whicher released her.

Five years later, Constance confessed to a priest that she had taken the child to the privy and killed him with her father's razor. The priest helped her inform the detective. Some believed Constance had mental problems and that her confession was false. Her father, Samuel Kent, was a known womanizer who had affairs with a nursemaid and then the nanny, whom he married (Constance's mother).

Constance was sentenced to death. The verdict was generally accepted but not the sentence. Newspapers, doctors and magistrates put pressure on the Home Secretary until he stayed the sentence. She served 20 years before her release in 1885 at the age of 41.

The next year, she emigrated to Australia to join her brother. She became a nurse and eventually matron of a nurse's home in New South Wales, dying in 1944 at the age of 100.

PRISON SHIPS

IF BRITISH PRISONERS DREADED being transported to Australia, a greater fear were the decommissioned warships anchored in mud at Woolwich on the Thames and in the Thames estuary, off the coast of Kent. These were permanent prison ships to relieve the shortage of space in Victorian prisons. Known as hulks, the rusty vessels, with names like *Defence* and *Success*, were overcrowded with long-term convicts and others awaiting transportation. Their quarters were infested with vermin, and many inmates died from diseases such as cholera and typhoid. Dangerous inmates were confined together in a box with bars known as the 'tigers' den'. Prisoners were released outside to work, but escapes were rare.

Left: The prison hulk *Warrior* in 1848. Its surgeon said inmates were too enfeebled by imprisonment to work on the dockyard.

The murder was such a sensation that Madame Tussaud's created a wax figure of Constance. Details of the case were used in 1868 by Wilkie Collins in *The Moonstone*, often regarded as Britain's first detective story. Charles Dickens also used elements of the story in his 1870 novel, *The Mystery of Edwin Drood*.

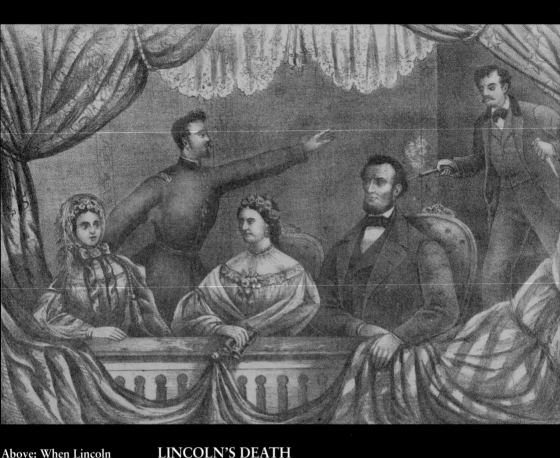

Above: When Lincoln
was assassinated, General
Ulysses Grant was
supposed to be with him
but instead decided to
visit his children.

LINCOLN'S DEATH

April 1865 brought the crowning achievement to Abraham
Lincoln. The 16th President of the United States had struggled
through four years of the Civil War with the South's rebelling
Confederate states. Then, on 3 April, the Confederate capital
at Richmond, Virginia, fell and Lincoln walked through its
streets. Even better, on 9 April the war ended with the surrender
of General Robert E. Lee to General Ulysses Grant. Wild
celebrations broke out in Washington, DC, as Lincoln took
cheers from his White House balcony.

On 14 April, Good Friday, the president attended a
performance of *Our American Cousin* at Ford's Theatre in
Washington, and was applauded enthusiastically as he entered
the president's box with his wife and another couple. This would
be his last hour, as John Wilkes Booth, an actor who supported
the South, crept up behind him with a derringer handgun and
fired a fatal shot to the back of his head. Booth then leaped to

the stage, shouting '*Sic semper tyrannis*!' ('Thus always to tyrants', Virginia's state motto.) The jump broke his leg. Many believed this was part of the play as Booth fled the building and escaped on a waiting horse.

Lincoln, 56, died the next morning in a nearby boarding house. Cavalry tracked the assassin to a barn on 26 April and reportedly shot him dead, though he may have committed suicide.

JOHN WILKES BOOTH

LINCOLN's assassin was born in Maryland, the son of a famous actor, Junius Brutus Booth, and younger brother of the renowned Shakespearean actor Edwin Booth. John Wilkes began acting at the age of 17 and was known for his rich voice and good looks.

When the Civil War began, his family remained Unionist but Booth supported the South without enlisting to fight. With the defeat of the Confederacy, he gathered together a few other conspirators and hatched a plan to kidnap Lincoln and swap him for Confederate prisoners. This failed when the president altered his schedule.

Booth now decided on a spectacular plot to assassinate Lincoln, Vice President Andrew Johnson and Secretary of State William Seward. Booth had the only success, with one accomplice stabbing but not killing Seward and four others in his house, and another plotter getting cold

feet about attacking the vice president. When Booth and his conspirator David Herold were cornered in a tobacco barn in Virginia, Herold surrendered but Booth refused. After the cavalry set fire to the building and a shootout occurred, they found Booth dying. 'Tell my mother I died for my country', he said. 'I thought I did for the best'. Looking at his hands, he muttered, 'Useless, useless'.

Right: Four conspirators in Lincoln's assassination were hanged on 7 July 1865, including Mary Surratt, the first woman executed by the government.

NED KELLY

Right: Ned Kelly shoots his way out of trouble, iron helmet protecting his head.

According to Australian opinion, Ned Kelly was either a vicious murderer or an Irish hero fighting against the oppressive British establishment. For its part, the Australian government today calls him one of the country's 'greatest folk heroes', who has had more books and songs written about him than any other historical Australian figure.

Ned's father was John 'Red' Kelly, a Catholic Irishman transported to Australia's penal colony for stealing two pigs. Edward 'Ned' Kelly was infuriated when his mother was arrested in 1878 for assaulting a policeman. He took to the impenetrable mountains of the Wombat Ranges with his brother Dan and two mates, Joe Byrne and Steve Hart. When four police tracked them down in 1878, Kelly's gang killed two and wounded another, resulting in an £8000 reward for their capture.

After several bank robberies, Kelly and his gang, wearing suits of steel armour, holed up in the Glenrowen Hotel, taking 60 hostages in that small town in Victoria. Police arrived and a shootout ensued, wounding its superintendent, Francis Hare, and other officers. The hostages were allowed to leave during a lull in the gunfire. Kelly was wounded in the arm and thumb but was able to retreat. Police killed his brother and the two other gang members, then burned the hotel down. At dawn, Ned reappeared to attack the police from the rear. After half an hour he was captured, shot in his legs not protected by the armour.

Tried and found guilty of the 1878 killing, Ned was sentenced to death. While in Melbourne Gaol, he wrote a letter protesting discrimination against poor Irish settlers. Some demonstrations were held to commute his sentence, but Kelly, 25, was hanged on 11 November 1880 at the gaol. His last words on the gallows were, 'Such is life'. He was buried in a wooden box in a mass grave holding the bodies of prisoners. His remains were identified by DNA in 2010, and Kelly was given a proper burial in 2013 next to his mother in the Victorian countryside he once terrorized. His grave is still unmarked to deter vandals.

WHEN FOUR POLICE TRACKED THEM DOWN IN 1878, KELLY'S GANG KILLED TWO AND WOUNDED ANOTHER, RESULTING IN AN £8000 REWARD FOR THEIR CAPTURE.

JACK THE RIPPER

Five prostitutes were murdered between August and November in 1888 in East London, and newspapers wrote sensational stories that first dubbed the feared killer 'Jack the Ripper'. These accounts also riveted readers in America and in Europe, where people were already unnerved by the numbers of anarchists and revolutionaries on the streets. Some London

Below: Ned Kelly's gang chose Anne Jones's Glenrowan Hotel for their last stand. The police burned it down to capture them.

reporters increased the number of victims to nine, and the police were not sure themselves. All of the prostitutes had been soliciting in the poor Whitechapel area and had their throats cut and bodies mutilated by someone who knew anatomy, supposedly a surgeon or a butcher.

Investigators generally agreed the five victims were Mary Ann Nichols on 31 August, Annie Chapman on 8 September, Elizabeth Stride and Catherine Eddowes on 30 September and Mary Jane Kelly on 9 November. The murderer inflicted abdominal mutilations on all but Stride. The worst damage was done to Kelly and he took her heart away. Other organs taken were Chapman's uterus and Eddowes's uterus and left kidney. Some investigators believed another murdered prostitute, Martha Tabram, was killed by the Ripper. Her death on 6 August would make her the first victim.

Police flooded the streets with extra constables and bloodhounds, bringing in hundreds of suspects who were soon released. One of the first, John Pizer, harassed prostitutes and was called 'Leather Apron' in the press because he wore one. Inspectors even photographed the retinas of one victim under the Victorian belief that a dead person's eyes would reveal the image of the last person she viewed, the murderer, but nothing was revealed.

As police struggled to close the case and calm a nervous public, someone claiming to be the killer began to send letters ridiculing their efforts. At the same time, a cardboard box addressed 'From Hell' was delivered to George Lusk, chairman of the Whitechapel Vigilance Committee. It contained half a kidney said to be from a victim; the writer claimed to have fried and eaten the other half, judging it 'very nise'. He closed with the challenge of 'Catch me when you can Mishter Lusk'.

Below: Many illustrations portrayed the horror of Jack the Ripper's murders in the gloomy backstreets of Whitechapel.

Opposite: The front page of the *Police News* used dramatic sketches to report the murder of Annie Chapman, the second victim.

THE ILLUSTRATED POLICE NEWS

LAW COURTS AND WEEKLY RECORD

No. 1,284.   SATURDAY, SEPTEMBER 22, 1888.   Price One Penny.

"IS HE THE WHITECHAPEL MURDERER?"

READY FOR THE WHITECHAPEL FIEND. WOMEN SECRETLY ARMED.

LATEST DETAILS OF THE WHITECHAPEL MURDERS

THE VICTIM LAST SEEN ALIVE

FORMAN OF JURY

Dr PHILLIPS

BROTHER OF VICTIM

I HAVENT THE MONEY FOR MY LODGING

SCOTLAND YARD OFFICIALS WATCHING THE CASE

CORONER

DETECTIVE THICKE

ANNIE CHAPMAN — BEFORE AND AFTER DEATH

A WHITECHAPEL SLAUGHTER YARD.

PAPER ON WHICH MURDERER WIPED HIS HANDS

LODGING HOUSE KEEPER

HANDKERCHIEF WORN BY VICTIM

THE BLOOD STAINS HANBURY ST

EXCITING SCENE IN BOSTOCK AND WOMBWELL'S MENAGERIE

MORE HORRIBLE MYSTERIES.

WHO WAS JACK?

SCOTLAND YARD NAMED FOUR **main suspects in 1889:**
• Aaron Kosminski, 23, a Polish Jew living in Whitechapel, who died in an insane asylum.
• Montague John Druitt, 31, a barrister and teacher who committed suicide.
• Michael Ostrog, 55, a Russian-born thief who had been in asylums.
• Dr Francis J. Tumblety, 56, an American 'quack' doctor arrested for indecency.

Other suggestions have been added through the years. Two often mentioned are:
• The painter Walter Sickert, who was fascinated by the killings.
• Prince Albert Victor, the son of King Edward VII and grandson of Queen Victoria, who wrote letters saying a prostitute had given him gonorrhoea.

FREDERICK DEEMING

Did Jack the Ripper settle in Australia in the Melbourne suburb of Windsor? Many in the country thought so after reading details of how Frederick Deeming killed his first wife and four children in Britain and his second wife in Melbourne.

Deeming was born in Leicestershire, married a Welsh woman, Marie James, and they had three girls and a boy. When his wife found out he was a bigamist, having married Helen Matheson, he murdered Marie and the children using a battle-axe and a knife, burying them under the fireplace with a cover of cement.

HE MURDERED MARIE AND THE CHILDREN USING A BATTLE-AXE AND A KNIFE, BURYING THEM UNDER THE FIREPLACE WITH A COVER OF CEMENT.

Using the alias of Albert Williams, he emigrated to Australia in 1891 with another wife, Emily. Immediately he bought cement and tools and started calling himself Mr Drewn. A month later, on Christmas Day, he murdered Emily and buried her the same way, under the fireplace and concrete. He disappeared and the owner of the house discovered the body by its sickening smell. The police found burned papers containing Deeming's real name and contacted English police, who told them about the first murders. With the killer on the run, newspapers published lurid stories about 'Mad Fred' being Jack the Ripper. By then Deeming was calling himself Baron Swanson and had another woman he intended to marry. Police intercepted his letters to her and tracked him to Western Australia, where he was captured. As they brought him home by train, crowds lined the route and shouted 'Murderer!' and 'Jack the Ripper!'.

Deeming's trial received massive international press coverage, with headlines in Britain, South Africa and America. He was found guilty and sentenced to hang. In Melbourne Gaol he wrote a book claiming to be Jack the Ripper, but the police doubted he was in London at that time. Deeming was executed on 24 May 1892 at the age of 38.

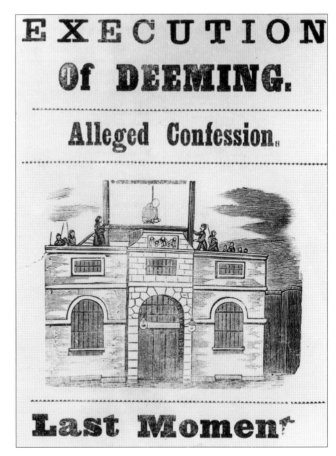

THE LAMBETH POISONER

Dr Thomas Neill Cream was a serial poisoner who killed women in Canada, the United States, England and probably Scotland. He was born in Glasgow and raised in Canada. After studying medicine in Montreal and London, he opened a practice in London, Ontario. Cream had married in 1876, and his wife died the next year after he aborted their child. In Canada in 1879 his pregnant lover died, killed by chloroform (the subject of Cream's university thesis).

Accused of murder, he fled to Chicago, where he performed illegal abortions for prostitutes. Four died, two by strychnine, and he tried to blackmail a pharmacist for the deaths. His only male victim, Daniel Stott, died in 1881 after his wife, Cream's mistress, supplied strychnine for his murder. To avoid jail, she implicated Cream, who was convicted and given a life sentence. His family bribed officials and he was released in 1891.

Above: Frederick Deeming's execution was covered by newspapers, booklets and sketches. For years his death mask was kept at Scotland Yard.

FATAL FACILITY; OR, POISONS FOR THE ASKING.

Child. "PLEASE, MISTER, WILL YOU BE SO GOOD AS TO FILL THIS BOTTLE AGAIN WITH LODNUM, AND LET MOTHER **HAVE** ANOTHER POUND AND A HALF OF ARSENIC FOR THE RATS (!)"

Duly Qualified Chemist. "CERTAINLY, MA'AM. IS THERE ANY OTHER ARTICLE?"

POISON OF CHOICE

VICTORIANS LIVED IN THE golden age of personal poisons. After all, lethal substances were hardly regulated because of their everyday use in many products such as wallpapers, fabrics and paints. This left murderers with abundant choice. Arsenic, tasteless and odourless, was the popular choice of poisoners. Used in cosmetics, it was easy to acquire and difficult to detect, since its effects looked like food poisoning. Cyanide was everywhere, and it could kill in seconds. This advantage was offset by its easy identification by the police. Strychnine remained popular with murderers, mainly because one could innocently purchase it for pest control.

Cream returned to London to set up a practice in Lambeth and began killing within two weeks. Two prostitutes died in October 1891 and two the next April, all from strychnine. Using different names, he tried to blackmail doctors threatening to accuse them of the crimes. Newspapers dubbed the killer 'the Lambert Poisoner'. Cream became the prime suspect when a New York policeman visited and he gave him detailed accounts of the victims. Scotland Yard contacted Chicago police, who revealed his prior conviction. Cream then made a critical mistake in telling police he knew who murdered Louisa Harvey, not knowing she was still alive after spitting out the strychnine-laced medicine he had given her.

On 3 June 1892, Cream was arrested and charged with the murders of four victims. He claimed his name was Dr Thomas Neill. On 21 October, Cream was found guilty and sentenced to death, being hanged on 15 November in Newgate Prison.

JOSEPH VACHER

France had its own Victorian serial killer, who was nicknamed 'the French Ripper'. Joseph Vacher, who was savage and cunning, went on a killing spree through rural France from 1894 to 1897, leaving more bodies than Jack had in London. As with coverage of the Whitechapel murders, French newspapers spread his fearful story throughout Europe and America.

Opposite: A cartoon in *Punch* magazine in 1849 takes a light look at the ease of purchasing poison.

Vacher, a former soldier, slaughtered at least 11 women and men, possibly 27. He showed the same sexual depravity as Jack the Ripper but, unlike the London crimes, the women were not prostitutes. His first victim, on 20 May 1894, was Eugenie Delhomme, 21, a mill worker near Beaurepaire in southeast France. She had been strangled, stabbed in the neck and her right breast mutilated. His later victims were adolescent farm workers, leading the newspapers to dub him 'the killer of little shepherds'. His most prominent victim was the Marquis de Villeplaine, murdered while walking in his park in southwestern France.

Vacher was tracked down by Emile Fourquet, the prosecutor from the town of Belley, who was the first to see a similar modus operandi and link the murders, since all victims had their throats cut and were mutilated, sometimes while still alive.

He then collected multiple eyewitness accounts to build up an early form of criminal profiling. Vacher had fled to Havana, where Fourquet tracked him down for the arrest.

Below: In the same way London journalists had covered Jack the Ripper, French newspapers sensationalized Joseph Vacher's reign of terror.

Le Petit Parisien

TOUS LES JOURS
Le Petit Parisien
5 CENTIMES.

SUPPLÉMENT LITTÉRAIRE ILLUSTRÉ

DIRECTION: 18, rue d'Enghien, PARIS

TOUS LES JEUDIS
SUPPLÉMENT LITTÉRAIRE
5 CENTIMES.

LE TUEUR DE BERGERS

At his trial in Bourg-en-Bresse, Vacher wore a hat made of white rabbit fur as a symbol of his purity. He had the misfortune of facing Dr Alexandre Lacassagne, a pioneer of forensic science and an expert in criminal psychology, who described Vacher's methods and mentality, rejecting his plea of insanity even though his first murder had occurred a month after his release from an insane asylum for an attempted suicide. Found guilty, Vacher was guillotined on 31 December 1898 at the age of 29.

AMELIA DYER

Britain's worst serial killer, Amelia Dyer, at first had seemed like a woman who was kind to mothers and loved their babies. She began her evil ways in the late 1860s in Bristol, where she was twice detained in mental asylums. She gave refuge to unwed mothers who gave her their babies when they left, a Victorian practice called 'baby farming'. But Amelia would kill them through starvation, smothering, strangulation or drugs. Amelia also served as a foster mother for infants, again killing them. Children often died young in the nineteenth century, but authorities became concerned about the deaths of those in her care. They charged her with child neglect, for which she served six months in prison in 1879. Amelia moved her criminal business to Reading in 1895, where she charged poor parents a fee to put their children up for adoption. As before, she murdered the children.

Above: Amelia Dyer's name reemerged in 2017 when packaging she had wrapped around a baby's body was discovered in a loft.

On 30 March 1896, a bargeman fished the body of baby Helena Fry from the Thames with white tape wrapped around her neck. Her body was in parcel paper

AMELIA WOULD KILL THEM THROUGH STARVATION, SMOTHERING, STRANGULATION OR DRUGS.

weighted down by a brick, and the paper contained Amelia's faintly written former name and address. This led police to her house on Kensington Road in Reading, where they found records of the adoption sham and arrested her. More infant bodies were discovered in the river. Fearing God's wrath, Amelia confessed

THE FIRST TO DIE WAS A TWO-MONTH-OLD BABY IN 1889, FOLLOWED TWO YEARS LATER BY A SIX-WEEK-OLD INFANT.

her crimes, telling police they could identify her dead babies 'by the tape around their necks' used to strangle them.

Her trial of the 'baby farming murders' became a sensation when it was estimated she had murdered about 400 infants. Newspapers dubbed Amelia 'the angel maker' and songs were sung about her. She pleaded insanity to no avail. Aged 57, she was hanged on 10 June 1896 at Newgate Prison. In the aftermath, the government initiated stricter supervision of adoption and child protection laws.

MINNIE DEAN

New Zealand had its own 'baby farmer' murderer, Williamina 'Minnie' Dean. Born in Greenock, Scotland, she had emigrated to New Zealand by 1862. Her daughter Ellen became depressed and drowned herself and her two children in a well. Since the late 1880s, Minnie had run a paid childcare business at her home, The Larches, in Winton, Southland. Up to nine children were under her care at any one time. The first to die was a two-month-old baby in 1889, followed two years later by a six-week-old infant. An inquest decided that Minnie had taken good care of them, but her premises were inadequate.

Police, however, began to observe her activities, so she began to advertise her service under false names. On 2 May 1895, a train guard noticed her boarding with a baby and a heavy hatbox, yet on the return journey only carried the hatbox. Police searched the track without success and then her garden, where they unearthed the remains of two babies, Dorothy Carter and Eva Hornsby, and a skeleton of a four-year-old boy. Minnie's trial for Dorothy's murder

Below: On the scaffold, Minnie Dean said 'Oh, God, let me not suffer', and her death was recorded as instantaneous.

THE CONDEMNED CHILD-MURDERER.

[BY TELEGRAPH.—PRESS ASSOCIATION.]
INVERCARGILL, 7th August.
Minnie Dean is to be executed next Monday morning.

The Southland Times states that the doomed woman was informed of the decision of the Executive on Saturday afternoon.

BAMBOO PUNISHMENT

CAPITAL PUNISHMENT WAS A universal sentence throughout the Victorian world, from hanging in the West to beheading in the Orient. The Chinese added various forms of physical punishment, including torture on the rack and the common sentence of bamboo beatings. For the latter, a prisoner was forced to kneel before a magistrate who decided how many strokes must be given. No one of any rank was considered exempt from flogging by bamboo. The smallest number of blows, for minor infractions, was five. The maximum of 100 blows was reserved for physicians who prescribed wrongly or domestics causing disturbance in the imperial palace.

Below: Even subordinates in the Chinese government were examined each year and given 40 blows if their work had not improved.

began on 18 June that year in Invercargill. The child had died from an overdose of the opiate laudanum, which was used to calm infants. Her defence said the baby's death had been accidental, but Minnie was convicted. Even Minnie's lawyer later wrote about her infamy 'sitting serene and unperturbed in a carriage with one tiny corpse in a tin box at her feet and another enshrouded in a shawl and secured by travelling straps in the luggage rack at her head'.

Minnie was hanged on 12 August 1895 at Invercargill Gaol, walking firmly to the scaffold and saying only 'I am innocent'. She is the only woman ever executed in New Zealand.

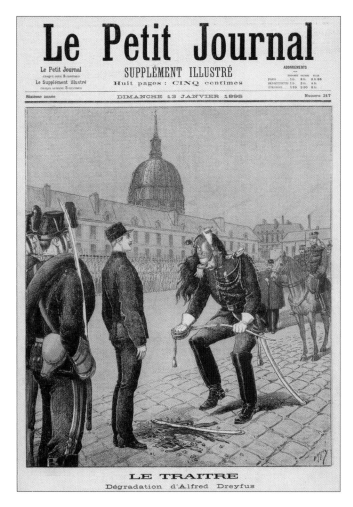

Le Petit Journal

SUPPLÉMENT ILLUSTRÉ

Huit pages : CINQ centimes

DIMANCHE 13 JANVIER 1895

LE TRAITRE

Dégradation d'Alfred Dreyfus

Above: The humiliation of Alfred Dreyfus was displayed in French newspapers, which a decade later had to report his innocence.

THE DREYFUS AFFAIR

The son of a wealthy Jewish textile manufacturer in France, Alfred Dreyfus joined the military and by 1889 was a captain in the War Ministry. In 1894, he was accused of spying for Germany and arrested. He was tried on flimsy evidence, convicted on 22 December for high treason and sentenced to life imprisonment. He was stripped of his rank and his sword symbolically broken. On 13 April 1895, Dreyfus was taken to Devil's Island, France's infamous prison off the coast of French Guiana in South America.

Dreyfus's trial had been suspect. French newspapers and many of the anti-Semitic public played up Dreyfus as the epitome of disloyal French Jews. However, evidence was found that a letter used to convict Dreyfus was written by another officer who was then tried and acquitted.

Among the many who questioned these legal manoeuvres were the famous novelist Emile Zola and Georges Clemenceau, a journalist and politician who would become France's premier during World War I. In 1898, Zola wrote a letter in Clemenceau's newspaper that was headlined 'J'Accuse' ('I Accuse'). It accused the Minister of War of covering up Dreyfus's wrongful conviction. Zola was tried, found guilty of libel and sentenced to one year in prison and a fine of 3000 francs.

The major with the letter that incriminated Dreyfus confessed his forgery and committed suicide in 1898. The next year, Dreyfus was returned from Devil's Island for a retrial and again found guilty on 9 September 1899 by court martial. France's new president pardoned him but many still considered him guilty. When he attended Zola's funeral in 1902, an assassination attempt wounded him. Another retrial occurred in 1904, and Dreyfus was found innocent. Parliament reinstated him in the army, decorated him with the Legion d'Honneur and he went on to fight in World War I. The affair had increased the campaign against anti-Semitism but seriously divided the country for years between right-wing nationalists and left-wing liberals.

LIZZIE BORDEN

Did Lizzie Borden take an axe and give her mother 40 whacks and her father 41? So goes the children's song, but reality was harder to determine. The motive seemed to be there, since her father Andrew and stepmother Abby were rich and disliked by

DEVIL'S ISLAND

THE MOST NOTORIOUS PRISON in history, Devil's Island was located on a tiny island off French Guiana on the northeast coast of South America. Napoleon III established it in 1854 for France's traitors, political dissidents and the most dangerous prisoners, who were given hard labour.

Alfred Dreyfus was kept in solitary confinement during his four and a half years there. When the prison closed in 1953, about 80,000 convicts had been held in Devil's Island. Some 50,000 had died from disease, hard labour, meagre food, executions by guillotine and escape attempts when they were drowned or eaten by sharks.

Left: The ruins of the Devil's Island prison were closed to the public for years, but tours are now available.

Lizzie and her sister, Emma, both in their 30s and still living at the family home in the small town of Fall River, Massachusetts. When their parents were brutally murdered on 4 August 1892, the sisters were set to inherit around $300,000 (worth about $8 million today).

Emma was away when the murders occurred, so Lizzie was the prime suspect. She had alerted the family maid, Bridget Sullivan, after finding her father's body that had been hacked as he slept on the sofa. Her stepmother was also mutilated in the family guest room. Sullivan, who was recovering from food poisoning, was briefly considered a possible suspect, as was a house guest, John Morse, brother of Lizzie's true mother. He had been gone at the time, so Lizzie was arrested and charged a week after the murder. Police noted she did not appear overly upset, and the house showed no sign of a break-in.

Lizzie waited in jail for 10 months before 'the trial of the century' began on 5 June 1893. The jury of 12 'mustachioed' men heard no evidence linking her directly to the murders. After 90 minutes, they acquitted her. Lizzie let out a cry of joy, sank in her chair, put her face in her hands, then gave another cry. The verdict split opinions across the nation: many were certain she had killed the two in a frenzy; others were equally sure a respectable lady from an upper-middle-class family could never commit such a grisly crime. No one else was ever charged.

Lizzie had no shame about her ordeal. She bought an expensive new house, Maplecroft, where her sister also lived until 1904. The next year, Lizzie changed her name to Lizbeth. This did not stop locals

Below: Lizzie Borden suffered for years under her vindictive father who once killed all of her pet pigeons with an axe.

from avoiding her in church and children tossing eggs and gravel at her house.

About a month after her trial, the children's sing-song rhyme appeared: 'Lizzie Borden took an axe and gave her mother 40 whacks. When she saw what she had done, she gave her father 41'. She died in 1927 at the age of 67. Her home is now the Lizzie Borden Bed and Breakfast Museum, often visited by crime fans and ghost hunters.

SHE HAD ALERTED THE FAMILY MAID, BRIDGET SULLIVAN, AFTER FINDING HER FATHER'S BODY THAT HAD BEEN HACKED AS HE SLEPT ON THE SOFA.

Left: Many locals at Borden's trial believed she was guilty, but the jury took only 90 minutes to find her innocent.

5

EMPIRE

The nineteenth century saw the unprecedented growth of
European powers and their military manoeuvring to consolidate
the explorations and colonial wars of the two previous centuries.
Having fought one another to settle and rule distant territories,
the European nations turned to strengthening their colonies.

MANY ADVANTAGES CAME from occupying an
undeveloped land that had weak defences.
Unequal trade agreements enriched the
colonisers, who could take away sought-after
raw materials and create new markets for their own goods.
Treasures and archaeological finds were usually removed by the
invaders. Overseas lands also served as useful military staging
points, as Hong Kong became when taken over by the British
in 1841. But colonial ventures were also fraught with dangers.
Spanish colonisation of the Americas eventually ended with its
costly defeat in the Spanish-American War in 1898. Discontent
and rebellion even plagued well-organized colonies whose people
were granted some freedom and self-government, as the British
experienced in India.

Opposite: Britain's
misconceived Charge of
the Light Brigade during
the Battle of Balaclava
saw Russian artillery
decimate the cavalry.

Above: This 1850 map of the British Empire shows the worldwide colonies and the diverse people under the British flag.

RULING THE WAVES

The British colonies were secured in different ways. Many came about from the pioneering work of chartered companies, such as the East India Company, the Hudson's Bay Company and the British South Africa Company. British officials, troops and settlers were found in all five continents, so the saying 'The sun never sets on the British Empire' was a proud boast.

When Victoria came to the throne in 1837, the Royal Navy depended on sailing ships somewhat like the ones with which Admiral Lord Nelson had won the Battle of Trafalgar in 1805. During her reign, Victoria witnessed the advent of ironclad ships, turbine engines, gun turrets and torpedoes. Britain's undisputed rule of the seas would last from after the Napoleonic Wars until

World War I. The average size of the Navy during the nineteenth century was 52,000 men, and the service was as powerful as the next two navies combined.

'THE SUN NEVER SETS ON THE BRITISH EMPIRE' WAS A PROUD BOAST.

Victoria's far-flung colonies would have been virtually impossible to maintain without the Royal Navy. Its impressive fleets actually ruled by fear, with no large sea battles and few shots fired in anger. On occasion, ships bombarded enemy cities, as when Canton was subdued in 1856 and Cairo in 1882. Most of the Navy's value lay in transporting troops, as during the Crimean War (also destroying the Russian Navy's Black Sea Fleet), the Indian Mutiny and the Boer Wars. Naval brigades even fought on land alongside the Army in some wars. At other times, it fought pirates off North Africa and in the South China Sea, and helped open such foreign markets as China and Japan. Worldwide admiration of the fleet came for its efforts to identify and capture the ships of slave traders. Among other worthy causes, the Navy surveyed oceans to produce navigation charts and explored new routes and coasts.

THE NORTHWEST PASSAGE

Captain Sir John Franklin in 1845 led an expedition with his flagship HMS *Erebus* and HMS *Terror* to find the Northwest Passage connecting the Atlantic and Pacific Oceans. His ships and crews were trapped in heavy sea ice on 12 September 1846. All disappeared, with the loss of all 129 men – the worst disaster in the Royal Navy's history of polar exploration. Search parties were conducted for 11 years before being called off, leaving one of the service's deepest mysteries unresolved.

Underwater archaeologists located the *Erebus* in 2014 and the *Terror* two years later. A crewman's scrawled note was also discovered in a stone cairn on King William Island. Dated 25 April 1848, it said that the ships had been abandoned three days earlier, adding that Franklin had died on 11 June 1847 and an officer named Crozier was now in charge of the surviving 105 sailors. They planned to follow Back's Fish River to safety at the Hudson's Bay Company. That's where the mystery returns.

THE OPIUM WARS

Two wars were fought against China's Qing Dynasty in the Victorian era, first in 1839–42 by the British and then in 1856–60 by an Anglo-French force. Both conflicts resulted in victories by the Western armies and led to China conceding territory and commercial rights as the dynasty was weakened from the onslaught. Having existed since 1644, it finally fell in 1912.

Trade was the reason China and Britain came to blows. Britain wished to end restrictions on foreign trade and high import duties, while China hoped to avoid free-trade agreements. The disagreement eventually centred on the opium trade, mostly conducted by the British; they were shipping the drug from India in return for tea from China. This created a massive number of addictions in all classes to the point of causing severe economic and social damage. China's balance of trade was also virtually ruined. When Queen Victoria was born in 1819, foreigners were bringing in some £5 million worth of opium each year for China's nearly three million opium users. After the death of Emperor Tao-kuang's son from an overdose, China's government prohibited its import and closed down opium parlours. In 1839, authorities in Canton seized and destroyed 20,000 chests containing 1400 tonnes of the drug.

Real conflict began in June 1840, when a British fleet arrived at Hong Kong and sailed up the Pearl River to open negotiations in Canton. When these failed, the force attacked and occupied the city in May 1841. Other British victories were won, including the capture of Nanking in August that led to the Treaty of Nanking on 29 August. The Qing Dynasty was forced to cede Hong Kong to the British, increase the ports of trade, including Shanghai, and pay British merchants for the opium destroyed. A second

Below: British troops take Hong Kong in 1841. It developed rapidly as an important trading centre under UK rule and was returned to China in 1997.

treaty on 8 October 1843 gave Britain a most-favoured-nation status with the right to try its subjects in its own courts. The following year, France and America gained the same agreements.

The Second Opium War, often called the Arrow War, began in October 1856 when Chinese officials in Canton boarded the *Arrow,* a ship registered in Britain. They arrested Chinese crew members for opium smuggling and reportedly lowered the Union Jack. In response, a British warship sailed to Canton, where it bombarded the city. In December, the Chinese in Canton burned foreigners' trading warehouses. The French, furious that one of their missionaries had been murdered in the country, joined the British, whose troops had been delayed by the Indian mutiny.

In 1857, the combined force captured Canton and replaced its governor. In April 1858, they reached Tianjin to force more treaties that opened even more ports to the Western traders, put foreign envoys in Beijing and gave freedom of movement to Christian missionaries. A later treaty legalized the importation of opium.

Above: The *Arrow* had a Chinese owner and was registered to fly the British flag but this had expired days earlier.

KINGS OF THE OPIUM TRADE

Two Scots, William Jardine and James Matheson, became wealthy shipping opium from India to China. Both graduated from Edinburgh University before forming their company and running a fleet of opium clipper boats. When Jardine heard of China's destruction of the 20,000 chests of the drug, he immediately went to the

British Foreign Secretary, Lord Henry Palmerston, and pressured him for action, providing maps and other information about China. Historians have credited the two Scots as the primary movers behind the opium wars.

Left: William Jardine studied at Edinburgh Medical School and first worked as a ship's surgeon with the British East India Company.

In June 1859, the peace was shattered when British ships were shelled by Chinese batteries at Dagu at the mouth of the Hai River, causing many casualties. When the Chinese refused to ratify the treaties, a larger force of warships with British and French troops destroyed the batteries in August 1860 and the following month captured Peking (now Beijing), burning the emperor's summer palace. The Chinese now signed the treaties to end the war and gave Britain the Kowloon Peninsula next to Hong Kong.

THE ANGLO–AFGHAN WARS

Two wars were fought in Afghanistan during Victoria's reign. When Britain was worried about Russian influence there, Britain used its Indian troops to secure control over that neighbouring country. The catalyst for conflict was British worry about Afghanistan's ruler, Dost Mohammad, who was playing off the two powers. The governor general of India, Lord Auckland,

ordered an invasion to restore the exiled Afghan ruler, Shah
Shuja. This force marched successfully to Kabul and in August
1839 installed Shuja as shah. Riots broke out against British
power and Dost Mohammad escaped from prison to lead
his followers in a battle against the British in Parwan on 2
November 1840. The following day he surrendered in Kabul and
was deported with his family to India.

Insurrections continued, however. On 6 January 1842,
the force of about 4500 British and Indian troops marched
back towards India, were ambushed by Afghans and virtually
destroyed in the Khyber Pass.

Russian influence continued to grow in Afghanistan and led
to the second Anglo–Afghan War. Dost's son, Sher Ali Khan,
now ruling, welcomed a Russian general in Kabul but refused
entry to Britain's envoy. This proved the last straw, and Lord
Lytton, the governor general of India, launched another invasion
on 21 November 1878. Sher Ali fled and died the next year in
exile. His son became emir as the British army occupied Kabul.
He allowed a permanent British presence there and promised
to conduct foreign affairs with British advice. On 3 September

Below: The attack on
the British Residency in
Kabul in 1879 provoked a
military response that led
to the emir's abdication.

1879, the British envoy and
his escort were murdered in
Kabul. Troops returned and
the throne was abdicated
until 1880, when Sher Ali's
nephew was crowned and
Britain and Russia drew
up the new boundaries of
Afghanistan.

A third Anglo–Afghan
War would occur after
Victoria's death when the
ruler, Amanullah, declared
independence from Britain,
beginning an inconclusive
war in 1919 that led to a
peace treaty that year.

one-eighth of the population, from starvation and disease.

The British government continued to allow grain to be exported from Ireland to Britain and permitted the importation of cornmeal (maize) from the United States to lessen the starvation. By 1847, some three million people were being fed at free soup kitchens. Although some poor relief was available, farmers became unable to pay rent and were evicted by landlords, many of them absentee British ones. Smallholders

Below: Even before the potato famine, many Irish farmers had long struggled in poverty on their small allotments.

WHO SENT RELIEF MONEY?

As IRELAND SUFFERED FROM famine, financial donations came from Britain and around the world, making this the first national disaster to attract international fundraising. Queen Victoria, the most generous single donor, gave £2000. The first funds came from British citizens in Calcutta, India, who raised £14,000. The Choctaw Nation of Native Americans sent $174. Other donations arrived from US President James K. Polk, US Congressman Abraham Lincoln, Pope Pius IX and Russian Tsar Alexander II. More came from the poor, with an orphanage in New York sending $2 and convicts on London's prison hulks raising small amounts.

were forced from their lands, which were consolidated into larger farms in fewer hands.

Opinions in Britain were not all sympathetic, with some blaming the famine on Irish families having too many children. The British government spent about £8 million on relief, but continued to import foods from Ireland, increasing local demand for Home Rule. Some Irish felt that the British had purposely extended the famine. About two million Irish emigrated, mostly to America and England. The country's population fell from 8.4 million in 1844 to 6.6 million in 1851. When it achieved independence in 1921, Ireland's population had halved.

THE CRIMEAN WAR

In 1854, a British and French force of some 125,000 men, along with troops from Turkey, invaded the Crimean Peninsula on the Black Sea to halt Russian expansion. Britain, France and Russia had been competing for influence in Turkey. Catholic France and Orthodox Russia sought to control access to religious sites in Bethlehem controlled by Turkey as part of the Ottoman Empire. In 1853 this had led to rioting in the city, and French monks killed several Orthodox ones. Russia's Tsar Nicholas I blamed Turkey, whom he called 'the sick man of Europe'.

FOLLOWING THE FAMINE, IRELAND'S POPULATION FELL FROM 8.4 MILLION IN 1844 TO 6.6 MILLION IN 1851.

On 2 July 1853, Russia invaded Moldavia and on 4 November destroyed the Turkish fleet on the Black Sea. The British and French declared war on Russia in March 1854 and with Turkish troops attacked with a poorly organized force of 60,000 to advance on Sevastopol. Field Marshal FitzRoy Somerset, Baron Raglan, commanded the British and often called his French allies 'the enemy' because he had fought them at Waterloo. Their combined forces first won an important battle at Alma on 20 September 1854, forcing the Russians to retreat.

> MEN SLEPT ON FILTHY FLOORS, RATS RAN FREELY, WATER WAS BAD AND NO PROPER TOILETS WERE AVAILABLE. THE PATIENTS ATE MOULDY BREAD AND OTHER OLD FOODS.

On 20 October, the enemies met at Sevastopol; the British besieged in atrocious weather, suffering heavy losses. They then attacked the Russian base at Balaklava, which five days later saw the tragic Charge of the Light Brigade taking heavy casualties from Russian artillery. On 5 November, the Russians made a surprise attack at Inkerman in fierce hand-to-hand fighting, but the British retained the field with help from the French. The Russians evacuated Sevastopol in September 1855 and the war ended the next spring.

The war was covered by William Howard Russell of *The Times*; he was the first famous war correspondent and later went to America to report on their Civil War.

'LADY WITH THE LAMP'

Florence Nightingale arrived with 38 nurses during a bleak time during the Crimean War. She took over the Barrack Hospital at Scutari, meeting resistance from Army doctors and staff. She called it the 'Kingdom of Hell', horrified at the lack of supplies and the unclean and crowded conditions; men slept on filthy floors, rats ran freely, water was bad and no proper toilets were available. The patients ate mouldy bread and other old foods. Many died of diseases contracted in the hospital.

Nightingale worked 20 hours a day to instigate a clean-up of the wards and the kitchen, even bringing in a French chef. She provided clean clothing and dressings and facilities for bathing.

THE CHARGE OF THE LIGHT BRIGADE

THE LIGHT BRIGADE, commanded by Major-General the Earl of Cardigan, consisted of light dragoons, hussars and lancers. The Light Brigade and Heavy Brigade made up the cavalry division commanded by Lieutenant-General the Earl of Lucan. When the order came on 25 October 1854 from Lord Raglan to advance rapidly to the front and keep the enemy from removing its guns, Cardigan led the charge of 673 cavalrymen along the valley. It was guarded from the heights on three sides by Russian artillery that bombarded them and, aided by infantry and cavalry, killed more than 100 and wounded about the same number. Only when the French cavalry charged in support was the Light Brigade saved from total destruction.

There was confusion about Raglan's order, since the Russian forces were also taking captured Turkish guns and repositioning them on the hills. Lucan, who hated Cardigan, failed to provide proper support from the rest of the cavalry. Raglan blamed him for the military blunder, and others said Raglan's message had been confused by Captain Louis Nolan who had delivered it to the cavalry.

The event in 'the valley of Death' was immortalized by Alfred, Lord Tennyson in his poem 'The Charge of the Light Brigade', written just weeks after the battle.

Below: One survivor recalled 'every man's features fixed, his teeth clenched and as rigid as death, still it was on – on'!

Right: Florence
Nightingale was named
for the Italian city of
her birth and grew
up in Derbyshire and
Hampshire.

THE PERRY PICTURES.   1820 —

FLORENCE NIGHTINGALE.

At night she walked through the wards with a lantern to sit with
dying soldiers and make sure others were comfortable, writing
letters for them to post home. The patients were soon calling her
'the lady with the lamp'.

After the war, Nightingale returned home a heroine and met
Queen Victoria and Prince Albert, telling them what changes
were needed in army hospitals. A Royal Commission was

LIFE IN THE BRITISH RAJ

THE BRITISH RAJ (Hindu word for 'rule') lasted from 1857 to 1947. The Victorian period highlighted the excesses of the British in India, who lived a life of privilege and luxury not possible back home. For those fortunate families, Westernization meant an exclusive British community protected from daily social contact with local people. Their exclusive clubs were off limits to Indians who were not servants. Other proper British amusements included tennis, polo matches, bridge parties and tea parties. Despite this, wives usually suffered from boredom, a lack of proper company and the extreme heat.

established based on statistics she had kept and her analyses. Patient deaths fell when military hospitals began to adopt her rules of cleanliness. She also published instructions still used today on taking care of the sick in households. In 1860, St Thomas's Hospital in London opened the Nightingale School of Nursing.

Nightingale had become weak from work and for her last 40 years was often bedridden, writing letters and collecting information for nurses. Having worked to establish modern nursing, Nightingale became the first woman to receive the Order of Merit in 1907. She died three years later.

HAVING WORKED TO ESTABLISH MODERN NURSING, NIGHTINGALE BECAME THE FIRST WOMAN TO RECEIVE THE ORDER OF MERIT IN 1907.

THE INDIAN REBELLION

The Indian Rebellion or Mutiny in 1857, also called the First War of Independence in that country, was a widespread uprising against British rule and Western ideas. It was carried out by sepoys, Indian soldiers in the army of the British East Indian Company Army, and is also known as the Sepoy Rebellion.

The first incident occurred on 29 March 1857 on parade grounds near Calcutta (now Kolkata), when a sepoy shot at a British officer and hit his horse. He was executed, along with another sepoy who had refused to arrest him. In April, sepoys in

Meerut refused to handle cartridges for their new Enfield rifles. The ends of the cartridges had to be bitten off, and they believed a rumour that they were lubricated with lard from cows and pigs, an insult to Hindus and Muslims. For their refusal, the men were thrown into prison in chains. In reprisal, their fellow soldiers shot their British officers on 5 May and marched to Delhi, where a sepoy garrison joined their rebellion. They also restored the retired Mughal emperor, Bahadur Shah II, to power.

The rebellion quickly spread through central and northern India, with some locals joining in. This required many British assaults; in Delhi, two British lieutenants sacrificed themselves blowing up the Kashmir Gate so the city could be taken. In June in Cawnpore (Kanpur), mutineers massacred the residents; they used knives and hatchets to kill all the women and children, who were thrown, dead or alive, into a well. The British took severe revenge on hundreds of sepoys, whom they bayoneted or even fired from cannons. At Lucknow, Sir Henry Lawrence and 1700 men defended the city from bombardment. Sir Henry was killed before the city was relieved in October by Sir Colin Campbell's troops.

Below: A 'siege train' of elephants hauled artillery during the Indian mutiny. Horses and camels were also used to transport the lumbering armies.

EMPRESS OF INDIA

IN A MOVE TO bind India closer to Britain, Prime Minister Benjamin Disraeli in May 1876 had Queen Victoria named Empress of India. Liberal politicians opposed this, but the flattered queen opened Parliament for the first time since Prince Albert's death to announce her new title. On 1 January 1877, the official proclamation and celebrations, complete with a 100-gun salute, were held in Delhi led by the Viceroy, Lord Lytton. Victoria never visited her 'Jewel in the Crown', but wore many Indian jewels and even had her Indian servant, Abdul Karim, teach her Urdu and Hindi, which she sometimes used for entries in her diary.

Below: The official celebration in Delhi was attended by British officials, foreign ambassadors, Indian nobility and 15,000 troops.

    Sir Hugh Rose commanded units that defeated the remaining rebels, including a difficult siege at Jhansi on 3–4 April 1858. Peace was declared on 8 July. The British response to the rebellion was to replace the East India Company with direct rule, reorganize the Indian Army and set up ways to better judge and react to Indian public opinion and needs.

THE GREAT EXHIBITION

PRINCE ALBERT SUGGESTED AN exhibition to demonstrate Britain's industrial achievements. This became the Great Exhibition, opened on 1 May 1851, the first ever international one for products. Victoria and Albert attended the opening ceremony in the Crystal Palace, the world's largest glass structure, built in Hyde Park for the displays. The Queen wrote how impressed she was with the vastness of the building, all its decorations and exhibits and the sound of the organ, adding that the visitors were 'all so civil and well behaved, that it was a pleasure to see them'.

Designed by Joseph Paxton, the structure was 563m (1848ft) long and 124m (408ft) wide. About 14,000 exhibitors took part. France sent the most products, and the displays highlighted the variety of the Empire's colonies, with the East Indies taking the most space. More than six million people – 40,000 a day – came before the closing ceremony on 15 October. Famous visitors included Charles Darwin, Lewis Carroll, Charles Dickens and Charlotte Brontë.

After the exhibition closed, the building was moved to Sydenham Hill (now part of southeast London) and reopened by the Queen in 1854. A fire destroyed it in 1936.

Below: Prince Albert received credit for the Great Exhibition, but Henry Cole of the Society of Arts suggested it to him.

THE NEW ZEALAND WARS

The New Zealand Wars were fought from 1845 to 1872 with Maori tribes against the government's British and colonial troops, including kupapa allies – Maori who fought on the British side. The estimated deaths were about 2000 Maori, 250 kupapa and 250 government soldiers. The government confiscated about one million hectares (2.5 million acres) from the warring Maori, although some property was later returned.

In 1839, Captain James Hobson had signed the Treaty of Waitangi as settlers fought to open the interior of the North Island. In 1843, a battle between Maoris and New Zealand Company settlers left four natives and 22 Europeans dead. The inconclusive Northern War ended in 1846, and an uneasy peace lasted during the 1850s. By 1858, New Zealand had more Europeans than native people, but Maori still held about 80 per cent of the North Island. That year, the first Maori king was crowned and began to unite tribes against selling their land. The greatest conflicts happened in the 1860s, including those between different Maori tribes. Governor George Grey gave Maoris

Above: When the Maori Wars had ended, the British punished tribes that had fought against the Crown by confiscating their land.

the opportunity to pledge allegiance to Queen Victoria before invading Waikato in July 1863. He sent some 12,000 imperial troops under Lieutenant-General Duncan Cameron to suppress fewer than 5000 warriors, and Europeans took firm control of New Zealand.

THE ANGLO–ASANTE WARS

The British fought four wars with the Asante Empire (now southern Ghana). The first, before Victorian years in 1823–31, was part of Parliament's anti-slavery campaign, intent on stopping countries from selling slaves. The British underestimated their opponent, whose slave trade had provided money to buy arms, so they withdrew after several defeats. Thirty years of peace followed.

Below: The 1902 picture 'The Bonnie Men Led the Advance' recalls the 1874 Battle of Amoaful during the Third Anglo–Ashanti War.

The second short war, in 1863–64, was initiated when the Asante occupied coastal provinces and encountered British troops. They clashed, suffering casualties on both sides. A request to London for more soldiers was turned down. Soon both sides were struck with illness and lost men, so fighting stopped in 1864 at a stalemate.

The third war, in 1873–74, came after Britain purchased the Dutch Gold Coast in 1871, which included the Asante claim on Elmina. Fearing they would have no access to the sea, the Asante invaded and took European missionaries as hostages. Sir Garnet Wolseley arrived in January 1874 with 2500 British troops. They fought successfully against the skilful Asante chief Amanquatia, who was killed. They then marched to the capital of Kumasi, confiscating many gold items now displayed in the British Museum. In July, the Treaty of Fomena ended the war, requiring the Asante to pay 50,000 ounces of gold and give up claims to Elmina.

The fourth war, in 1895–96, was brief. Worried about French and German designs on the country's gold, the British invaded in December 1895 using the pretext of the Asante failing to meet the stated reparations (only 4000 ounces were paid). The troops marched to Kumasi without resistance and deposed the Asante leader Asantehene, ending the war. In 1902, Asante was declared a British crown colony.

ATTACK ON ABYSSINIA

In 1867, King Theodore II of Abyssinia (now Ethiopia) wrote to Queen Victoria and others to request British military help against his Muslim enemies and for technicians to modernize his country. When this was ignored, he imprisoned the British consul along with missionaries and civilians. In 1868, Lieutenant-General Sir Robert Napier led a punitive expedition of 13,000 soldiers over 640km (400 miles) of difficult land to the king's mountain stronghold at Magdala, where he waited with an army of 9000 men.

The two sides clashed on 10 April and Napier's better-armed force decidedly defeated the Abyssinians. The British lost 20 men and the Abyssinians 2200.

With this defeat, Theodore released his hostages and sent along a peace offering of cattle. Napier took this as a surrender and promised to treat the royal family with dignity. Theodore replied that he had no intention of surrendering, which provoked a British bombardment. Wounded in one leg, Theodore committed suicide, shooting himself in the mouth with a revolver Queen Victoria had presented to him in 1854 and inscribed 'as a slight token of her gratitude'.

Below: The suicide of Theodore ended his life of violent moods. During one angry spell, he executed 7000 prisoners of war.

THE ZULU WAR

The British wished to take over Zululand in order to establish a South African federation of British colonies and Boer republics. British rule was not acceptable to the Zulu king, Cetshwayo, who formed an army of up to 60,000 men, mostly armed with spears and shields. When news of this reached Sir Bartle Frere, the British high commissioner for southern Africa, he demanded that Cetshwayo break up his army within 30 days. When the king ignored this ultimatum, Frere in January 1879 sent troops commanded by Lieutenant-General Lord Chelmsford.

On 22 January, Chelmsford advanced, leaving one-third of his troops encamped but poorly defended at Isandlwana. Cetshwayo ordered his 20,000 men to 'March slowly, attack at dawn and eat up the red soldiers'. They killed some 800 British soldiers and 500 African auxiliary troops, carrying away nearly 1000 rifles and ammunition. Another Zulu force of 4000 later that day attempted a surprise attack on the British depot at Rorke's Drift, but the troops had been warned by survivors from Isandlwana. In a 12-hour engagement, 120 soldiers shot more than 500 Zulu warriors.

Colonel Evelyn Wood then attacked and won a victory at Khambula on 29 March, killing some 3000 Zulus; Chelmsford's men then killed more than 1000 at Gingindlovu. His force continued to Ulundi where, on 4 July 1879, they used Gatling guns and artillery to kill 6000 charging Zulus while losing only 10 soldiers. They also captured Cetshwayo, who was sent into exile in Cape Town and later London.

Below: The French artist Alphonse de Neuville painted 'The Defense of Rorke's Drift' in 1880, a year after that British victory.

LOUIS-NAPOLEON

THE FRENCH PRINCE IMPERIAL, Louis-Napoleon, was exiled in London when the Zulu War began. He requested to join the expedition and this was allowed after the intervention of Queen Victoria and Empress Eugenie, with the understanding that he would be kept from danger. The prince was assigned to Lord Chelmsford's staff and on 1 June 1879 set out on a reconnaissance patrol near Ulundi, escorted by seven men. Zulus attacked and he fell when his saddle strap broke. One companion was killed and the others escaped. Louis-Napoleon ran, pursued by seven Zulus who overtook and killed him with 18 spear wounds.

Above: The death of Louis-Napoleon was dramatically captured in 1882 by the French painter Paul Joseph Jamin.

THE BOER WARS

The first Boer War of 1880–81 in South Africa saw the Boers (Afrikaners) of the Transvaal revolt against Britain's 1877 annexation. It began on 16 December 1880 when Boer forces lay siege to British garrisons in several towns, including Pretoria, Rustenburg and Marabastad. The British failed in initial attempts to break the Pretoria siege and to invade the Transvaal. On 26 December, 400 men under Major-General Sir George Pomeroy Colley occupied the towering Majuba Hill overlooking the Transvaal border. The Boers stormed their position on 27 February 1881 and killed five officers, including Colley, and 87 men, losing only one man themselves. Peace came with the Pretoria Convention of 3 August 1881, but failed to provide independence for the Transvaal. This finally came at the London Convention of 27 February 1884.

Above: Boer fighters dig in at Ladysmith, South Africa, before British troops forced their retreat in 1900.

Called the Boer War, Second Boer War, Anglo–Boer War or South African War, this second conflict lasted from 1899 to 1901 and pitted Britain, who ruled the colonies of the Cape and Natal, against the two Boer colonies of the Transvaal and the Orange Free State. The British forces numbered nearly 500,000 men to the Boers' 88,000. The key British interests involved empire building and control of the gold mines of the Transvaal.

The Boers refused to grant citizenship to settlers who were not Boers, most being British. On 11 October 1899, they warned Britain to halt building up military forces. As tensions mounted, the Boers invaded the British colonies of the Cape and Natal and defeated their troops, taking several main towns during 'Black Week' on 10–15 December. In February 1900, British reinforcements overwhelmed the enemy and by June had relieved Ladysmith, Kimberley, Johannesburg and Pretoria. Britain then annexed the Transvaal and the Orange Free State.

The war seemed over in October, but the Boers took up guerrilla warfare to raid army units, steal supplies and disrupt communications. In February 1901, General Kitchener, the British commander in chief, offered compromises to secure peace. Among these were the republics becoming crown colonies with ultimate self-government, an amnesty, a required compensation fund and 'coloured persons' given legal rights and the vote in the future that would be limited 'to secure the just predominance of the white race'. Terms were accepted in May 1902 with the Peace of Vereeniging and the compensation set at £3 million.

The war was the first European conflict that employed modern twentieth-century weapons such as machine guns and high explosives. It was also one of the first to introduce concentration camps for civilians.

CONCENTRATION CAMPS

As BOER GUERRILLAS ATTACKED, the British created concentration camps confining about a sixth of the Boer population. It was hoped the desire to reunite their families would lead to surrender. They herded in civilians, especially women and children, from about 3000 farms and houses burned in the army's 'scorched earth' policy that also saw crops burned and livestock killed.

Some 115,000 Boer civilians were confined together in 1901–02; almost 30,000 died from disease and hunger, about 22,000 of these being children. Blacks were also confined to camps, where some 20,000 died while being used as labour for gold mines. These tragedies were caused by a lack of supplies, poor administration and little concern for those confined.

In 1900, Emily Hobhouse launched the South African Women's and Children's Distress Fund and travelled from England to tour the concentration camps in Port Elizabeth, Johannesburg, Bloemfontein and other sites. She recorded that 50 children a day were dying in the overcrowded and unhygienic camps. Her reports said the inmates had no soap, inadequate water, no beds or mattresses, scarce fuel, meagre rations and all kinds of sicknesses, including measles, bronchitis, pneumonia, dysentery and typhoid. Her criticisms and campaign for changes helped undermine British support for the war.

Above: A member of the Liberal Party, Emily Hobhouse spoke out to denounce activities of the British government in South Africa.

CONQUERING EGYPT

By 1876, a commission of European powers appointed Britain and France to jointly control Egypt's treasury, customs, ports, railways and post offices. This was because the ruling Khedive Ismail Pasha had run up debts of nearly £100 million. The rights given the two colonial powers angered the Egyptians, still part of the Ottoman Empire. A new ruler, Khedive Tawfiq, took over and in 1881 a National Party was formed asking for 'Egypt for the Egyptians' with an army led by Ahmad Urabi Pasha Al-misri.

On 19 and 20 May 1882, a joint British and French fleet anchored off Alexandria, worried about access to the Suez

THE SUEZ CANAL

CONSTRUCTION OF THE CANAL that links
the Mediterranean to the Red Sea began
in 1859 by the Suez Canal Company, a
French concern. It first used forced peasant
labour digging with picks before Europeans
employed large machinery. The official
opening of the 164km (102 mile) canal
was on 17 November 1869. Britain, first
opposing the waterway's construction as a
scheme to overtake its shipping dominance,
bought a 44 per cent share for £400,000
in 1875. It was the only maritime power
that refused to sign the 1888 Convention of
Constantinople opening the canal to ships of
all nations. (It eventually signed in 1904.)

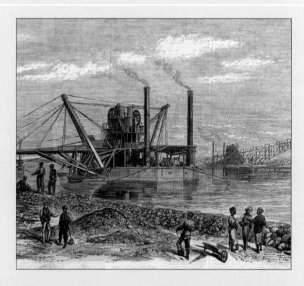

Above: The canal was built with eight major bends
and utilized several lakes along the way.

Canal. Rioting broke out in the city on 11 June, in which several
hundred were killed, including 50 foreigners. When the Egyptians
refused to remove cannons brought in to defend the city, the
French withdrew but the British bombarded Alexandria with
all 15 Royal Navy ships being engaged. Two days later, British
troops entered the partially destroyed city and Tawfiq sought
their protection, leaving Urabi in charge of the country.

In July and September, 31,000 more troops arrived under
Lieutenant-General Sir Garnet Wolseley and occupied Cairo as
40 warships secured the canal. Some minor engagements took
place and on 13 September British forces, led by the Highland
Brigade with its bagpipers, won an intense battle that lasted over
an hour at Tel-el-Kebir. This was followed by a march to Cairo,
where Urabi was taken prisoner and exiled to Sri Lanka, while
Tawfiq was restored to power.

British troops remained in Egypt, which was part of the
British Empire, until 1942.

Opposite: British horse
artillery move their guns
during the Egyptian
campaign in 1882 to
control access to the
Suez Canal.

EUROPEAN EMPIRES

WHILE THE MIGHTY BRITISH Empire was circling the globe, other European powers were carving out their share of colonial rewards. France, Germany, Russia and Austria-Hungary all developed empires of their own.

After being stripped of its overseas possessions following the Napoleonic Wars, France began rebuilding its colonial presence in the early nineteenth century. France took over Algiers in 1830, and later established protectorates in Tunisia and Morocco, giving it control of both shores of the Western Mediterranean. Wishing to gain a foothold in Asia, France sent warships to Vietnam, supposedly to protect its missionaries. In 1858 a French fleet bombarded Tourane (now Da Nang), killing some 10,000 people, and a year later captured Saigon (now Ho Chi Minh City). French Indochina, which also included Cambodia, was established in 1887, and Laos was added in 1893.

Germany came late to the imperial race, after only achieving unification in 1871. With nationhood, however, came the desire for colonial acquisitions. In the early 1880s, with prime lands already controlled by other European powers, Germany looked to Africa. German Togoland (now part of Togo and Ghana), Cameroon, German East Africa (now Rwanda, Burundi and Tanzania) and German South-West Africa (now Namibia) were all established. Unlike other European nations, Germany profited little from its colonies, sending settlers there rather than exporting raw materials.

The Russian Empire expanded in Asia during the nineteenth century. Before Victoria came to the throne, Georgia had united voluntarily with Russia in 1801, Persia had ceded Azerbaijan in 1813 and an Armenian province in 1828. However, many peoples resisted. The Chechens fought against Russian occupation from 1834 to 1859. Russian rule came to Kazakhstan in the 1840s, and, after fierce resistance, to Circassia in the Caucasus Mountains from 1860 to 1864, with the forced removal of the entire population.

The Austro-Hungarian Empire came about peacefully with the 1867 Ausgleich ('compromise') that established a dual monarchy for the two countries. The year before, Austria had lost the seven-week Austro-Prussian War, which led to it being expelled from the German Confederation. Austria sought an alliance with the Hungarians, who were given full internal autonomy. Austria's Emperor Franz Joseph and future monarchs would rule the 'common monarchy' as emperor of Austria and king of Hungary. The Hapsburg Empire was divided into two states: Cisleithania – comprised Austria, Bohemia, Moravia, Slovenia, Austrian Poland and Silesia; and Transleithania – included Hungary, Croatia and Transylvania.

FESTIVAL OF THE BRITISH EMPIRE

Queen Victoria's Diamond Jubilee in 1897 celebrated her 60 years on the throne. It had the theme of 'Festival of the British Empire' at the suggestion of Colonial Secretary Joseph Chamberlain. The Empire was at its height, embracing 450 million people on every continent and still growing. Since 1870 it had added Kenya, Rhodesia, Uganda, Cyprus, Zanzibar, Fiji, the New Hebrides, Somaliland and Bechuanaland.

Jubilee Day on 22 June, a Tuesday, was lavishly celebrated throughout Britain and around the world. Rulers and representatives from all the colonies were invited to London to participate. In the morning, Victoria sent a telegram to every country in the Empire, saying 'From my heart I thank my beloved people. May God bless them'. In return, she received 1310 telegrams of congratulations. The previous autumn, she had become the longest-reigning monarch in British history.

The grand procession with the 78-year-old queen, still dressed in mourning black, was led by colonial troops that included Indian Lancers, Canadian Mounties and Australian Cavalry. Soldiers included survivors of the Charge of the Light Brigade. All passed massive crowds of enthusiastic spectators on the way from Buckingham Palace to St Paul's Cathedral for an open-air memorial service, during which the queen sat in her open carriage because of her rheumatism. She later wrote: 'No-one ever, I believe, has met with such an ovation as was given to me, passing through those six miles of streets...The crowds were quite indescribable and their enthusiasm truly marvellous and deeply touching. The cheering was quite deafening and every face seemed to be filled with joy. I was much moved and gratified'.

In the evening, buildings were outlined in lights, fireworks exploded and beacons flamed around the country. On this and the next two days, street parties and concerts were held in most British towns, with London giving 400,000 meals to poor residents and Manchester providing 100,000 for theirs.

Below: The reverse side of a commemorative medal issued in 1897 for the Diamond Jubilee of Victoria, Queen and Empress of India.

6

AMERICA

Victorian America reflected many values of the Old Country, from morals to architecture. The working class, unfortunately, were just as poor pursuing their American Dream. Both countries expanded: Britain created an overseas empire, while America pushed west for more land.

HORACE GREELEY, editor of the *New York Tribune*, was credited in 1851 with urging 'Go west, young man, go west'. Americans hardly needed his advice, as pioneers travelled to acquire cheap land with the protection of cavalry that defeated any Native Americans who stood in their way. A bigger incentive in the West for speculators was gold; this led to the California Gold Rush of 1848–51.

None of these events compared to the tragedy back east that dominated the second half of the nineteenth century. The Civil War between Union and Confederate states was brought about by the slave-holding South's desire to establish its own nation. The resulting conflict would kill more Americans than any other war.

Opposite: John D. Rockefeller founded Standard Oil, becoming the world's richest man. The company's monopoly led to the 1890 Antitrust Act.

ROBBER BARONS

As in Britain, the Victorian era in America saw an explosion of industry and wealth. Dozens of strong-willed men made enormous wealth by monopolizing specific industries and businesses that created jobs and drove the economy to new heights. They were admired as 'captains of industry', but have become known as 'robber barons' for exploiting their workers and engaging in unethical business practices, such as fraud, conspiracy, intimidation and corruption. Six who became wealthy and powerful in this way were:

John Jacob Astor, born in Germany as Johann Jakob Astor, was the richest person in America when he died in 1848, worth more than $110 billion in today's money. His fortune was made trading fur, having founded the American Fur Company in 1808 and shipping to Europe and even China. He made his greatest wealth investing in real estate in New York City. He bequeathed $400,000 to build the city's Astor Library, which in 1895 became the New York Public Library.

Andrew Carnegie, born in Scotland, became rich in America managing railroads. He then invested in ironworks that supplied Union soldiers during the Civil War. In 1901, he sold Carnegie Steel to J.P. Morgan for $487 million, making him the world's richest man. He was one of the most generous philanthropists, saying 'A man who dies rich dies disgraced'. He funded libraries, universities, theatres and scientific research.

J(ohn) P(ierpont) Morgan was a financier with the skill of organizing various industries, such as the railroads and steel. He was a partner in the New York firm that was the main source financing the US government. In 1892, he arranged the merger that created General Electric. In 1895, his firm became J.P. Morgan and Company, one of the world's greatest banking houses. After buying Carnegie Steel in 1901, he added mergers to create the world's first billion-dollar corporation, the United States Steel Corporation.

John D(avison) Rockefeller monopolized America's oil industry, founding Standard Oil. He used deals with railroads for cheap delivery rates to drive competitors out of business. By 1890, his trust controlled some 90 per cent of the country's petroleum production. He became the first American worth $1 billion and was the world's richest man. Late in his life, he turned to philanthropy, giving some $500 million to worthy causes, including establishing the University of Chicago in 1892.

Below: Cornelius Vanderbilt was the son of a poor farmer. He left school at age 11 to work on the docks.

Cornelius Vanderbilt, nicknamed 'Commodore', became a shipping and railroad magnate. He began his own steamship company in 1829 and was a millionaire by 1846. In the 1850s, he invested in early railroads, providing the first rail service from New York City to Chicago in 1873. That year, he made a $1 million endowment to found Vanderbilt University in Nashville, Tennessee. Vanderbilt's personal fortune was worth $100 million.

E(dward) H. Harriman was a broker with the New York Stock Exchange in 1870 and decided to invest in railways. In the 1890s he acquired the Union Pacific Railroad and eventually controlled five railways, a steamship company and Wells Fargo Express Company. He led an expedition of scientists to Alaska in 1899 to explore and map the region, where the Harriman Fjord and Harriman Glacier were named in his honour. In 1904, US President Theodore Roosevelt sued Harriman about his monopoly and the Supreme Court forced him to break up his railroad empire.

THE TRAIL OF TEARS

In one of the worst chapters in United States history, the US government under Presidents Andrew Jackson and then Martin Van Buren carried out the removal of about 100,000 Native Americans from the southeast to reservations in the Indian Territory (now Oklahoma). They mostly included the Cherokee but also the Choctaw, Chickasaw, Creek and Seminole. Their round-up began in May 1838 in Georgia (where gold had been found on their land), Tennessee, North Carolina and Alabama. The forced march of about 8120km (5045 miles) was known to the Native Americans as 'the trail where they cried'.

Below: 'The Trail of Tears', a 1942 painting by American artist Robert Lindneux, captures the agony of the Cherokee nation's removal.

Beginning in October through a harsh winter, the long journey by foot of nearly 17,000 Cherokee, often without shoes, caused some 4000 deaths. US troops pushed them rapidly forward without allowing them to treat the sick or bury the dead. The last group arrived in March 1839 led by Chief John Ross, who was of Scottish and Cherokee descent. About 13,000 had first been held in military stockades because of a drought, and some 1500 died there. Another 800 deaths occurred that year after they reached their new homes.

THE US GOVERNMENT CARRIED OUT THE REMOVAL OF ABOUT 100,000 NATIVE AMERICANS FROM THE SOUTHEAST TO RESERVATIONS IN THE INDIAN TERRITORY

About 1000 Cherokees avoided the removal from Tennessee and Georgia. In 1868, they established their government in Cherokee, North Carolina, and their descendants still live there.

THE MEXICAN WAR

Also called the Mexican–American War, the conflict was caused when the United States annexed Texas in 1845 and a dispute continued over where the Texas–Mexico border lay. US President James Polk sent a representative to Mexican President José Herrera to offer $30 million for what is now California and New Mexico. Herrera refused to see him, so Polk sent General Zachary Taylor to occupy the disputed Texas border. On 25 April 1845, Mexican troops crossed the Rio Grande and killed some of Taylor's men. On 13 May, the US Congress declared war on Mexico.

Leading the Mexican Army was General Antonio López de Santa Anna, who had led the slaughter of Texans and others at the Alamo in 1836. He was released from exile in Cuba by President Polk, who sent a ship to convey him to Mexico to negotiate peace. Instead, Santa Anna took over the Mexican forces. During the war, American soldiers would shout 'Remember the Alamo!' during battles.

Fighting began when Taylor's army crossed the river to capture and plunder Monterrey. He also won a victory against a large Mexican force at the Battle of Buena Vista on 22–23

Above: During the Battle
of Buena Vista, the
furious fighting left 3400
Mexicans dead or injured
to only 650 Americans.

February 1847. At the same time, General Winfield Scott
went by sea to capture Veracruz after a three-week siege and
on 14 September 1847 marched into Mexico City, which fell
immediately. US deaths had numbered about 1500 and disease,
especially yellow fever, had killed at least 10,000 men.

The one-sided Treaty of Guadalupe Hidalgo ended the war
on 2 February 1848. For a payment of $15 million, Mexico
lost almost half of its territory as it ceded more than 1,300,000
square kilometres (500,000 square miles), nearly all of the areas
now forming the states of Arizona, New Mexico, Nevada, Utah,
California, Texas and western Colorado.

Taylor became a hero and in 1848 was elected president after
Polk. Many of those who would become generals in the Civil
War 13 years later took part in the Mexican War, including
Robert E. Lee and Ulysses S. Grant. The latter called the war
against Mexico 'one of the most unjust ever waged by a stronger
against a weaker nation'.

THE CALIFORNIA GOLD RUSH

Gold was discovered in California on 24 January 1848 at Sutter's Mill near Sacramento. The next year, the population had jumped from about 14,000 to 100,000 and California had hurriedly become a state. By 1852, some 250,000 lived there. These victims of gold fever became known as 'the Forty-niners', and they were followed by various hustlers, card sharps, prostitutes and violent hell-raisers.

When the cry of 'Gold!' was heard, one newspaper wrote, 'the field is left half planted, the house half built, and everything neglected but the manufacture of shovels and pickaxes'. These prospectors began by panning tiny pieces of gold from streams before companies organized to sink shafts to reach the precious metal. The big rush had ended by the end of the 1850s, but at the end of the century two mines, the Mother Lode and Kalmath, had produced gold worth $25 billion in today's equivalent.

Besides California, other strikes were found in Colorado in 1858 near Pike's Peak and in Nevada in 1859, where the Comstock Lode also contained silver. Congress created both lands as territories in 1861. More gold and silver combined

> WHEN THE CRY OF 'GOLD!' WAS HEARD, 'THE FIELD IS LEFT HALF PLANTED, THE HOUSE HALF BUILT, AND EVERYTHING NEGLECTED BUT THE MANUFACTURE OF SHOVELS AND PICKAXES'.

MANIFEST DESTINY

THE MEXICAN WAR was a large step in America's Manifest Destiny, the doctrine used to explain the country's inevitable expansion west across the continent. It included the Louisiana Purchase in 1803 from France, an acquisition of 2,144,520 square kilometres (828,000 acres); and was later used to promote the Spanish–American War and the further acquisitions of Alaska (1867) and Hawaii (1898) from Russia.

The term was first used in 1845 by an editor, John L. O'Sullivan, from the Democratic Party, who wrote about 'the fulfilment of our manifest destiny to overspread the continent allotted by Providence for the free development of our yearly multiplying millions'.

#357. "We have It Rich." - Washing and
panning gold. Rockerville, Dak.
Old-timers, Spriggs,Lamb and Dillon at work.
Photo and copyright by Grabill, 1889.

Above: Most 49ers
rushing to California had
to pan for gold in streams,
a backbreaking job with
few rewards.

were found in 1874 at Deadwood in the Black Hills of South
Dakota territory (on Dakota Sioux land) and in 1891 at Cripple
Creek, Colorado.

COMMODORE PERRY

Matthew C. Perry had already served in the War of 1812 and the
Spanish–American War when he turned his efforts to Japan. On
8 July 1853, he sailed his US squadron into Uraga harbour at
the entrance to Edo (now Tokyo) Bay to convince the Japanese
to open their country to American trade. Since the Japanese had
no naval force, Commodore Perry could use his military power
if needed. He refused an order to leave and threatened force
to deliver his letter from President Millard Fillmore requesting
diplomatic relations and a treaty.

The Japanese called his fleet of two frigates and two sailing
vessels 'black ships of evil mien', but the following year the ruling

DEADWOOD

WHEN GOLD WAS DISCOVERED in Deadwood, it lured more than prospectors. Some of the Wild West's most legendary desperadoes stayed awhile, including Wild Bill Hickok and Calamity Jane, who spent weeks there. They arrived in 1876 in the wagon train of Bill's friend, Colorado Charlie Utter, accompanied by some 100 prospectors, gamblers and 'working girls'.

James Butler Hickok, known as Wild Bill, was a gambler and gunslinger famed for killing several men while sheriff of Hays City, Kansas, and marshal of Abilene, Texas. During the Civil War, he was a Union scout, sharpshooter and spy. He was killed playing poker on 2 August 1876, shot in the back by Jack McCall. Hickok had been holding a poker hand of pairs of aces and of eights. This became known to poker players as 'the dead man's hand'.

Martha Jane Canary, nicknamed Calamity, took pride in wearing men's clothes and presenting a rough nature,

cursing, spitting tobacco and guzzling beer. She professed love for the married Wild Bill, who regarded her only as a close friend. She married in 1891, four years later joined Buffalo Bill's Wild West Show and in 1901 appeared at the Pan-American Exposition. Calamity then returned to Deadwood and died in 1903.

Right: Wild Bill Hickok's exploits, real and imaginary, were sensationalised in dime novels, making him a legend of the Wild West.

Shogun signed a treaty that allowed diplomatic relations and permitted the United States to trade at two ports. This was done with reluctance and remembrance of what had befallen China in the opium wars. However, after indications that Japan's defences were being increased, Perry returned with nine ships to Edo harbour. On 31 March 1854, the two countries signed their first treaty, the Treaty of Kanagawa, which allowed more American trading privileges and additional diplomatic agreements. After these successes, other nations – Britain, Russia, France and Denmark – also signed treaties to receive trading advantages.

Perry had exposed the weakness of the Shogun government's 200-year isolation, and it eventually collapsed, giving formal control to the Emperor and paving the way to modernization.

THE KNOW-NOTHING PARTY

Below: Commodore Matthew Perry's force landed in Japan in 1853. Later he advised the US government to occupy Pacific islands.

Despite being children of immigrants, many Anglo-Saxon Protestants born in America turned against later immigrants and Catholics, whom they felt owed allegiance to the Pope. The Native American Association (not meaning Indians) was formed in 1837, followed by the secret Order of the Star Spangled Banner in 1849, which became the American Party in 1854. The

latter was popularly called the Know-Nothing Party because of its secrecy with passwords and hand signals, and its members being instructed to say 'I know nothing' when asked about their meetings and actions.

The Know-Nothings campaigned for the exclusion of immigrants and Catholics from voting and public office. Their party made an immediate impact in 1855, winning local and state elections and eventually sending more than 100 new members to the US Congress as well as electing eight governors. This success was short-lived; the next year, at its 1856 convention, pro-slavery delegates took control. The party declined and never recovered when the nation's attention turned to the Civil War in 1861 and American-born soldiers fought alongside new immigrants and Catholics in both the Union and Confederate armies.

Below: Slaves were overworked and often mistreated, with owners breaking up families to sell children to other slaveholders.

SLAVERY

The institution of slavery was well established in the United States by the Victorian period. The British had first shipped slaves to the West Indies and America in the 1600s, and New England slave merchants had picked up the trade soon after. George Washington, Thomas Jefferson and other founding fathers of the United States owned slaves. All of the northern states had banned slavery by 1804, and three years later the British Parliament banned the trade. In 1808, the US Congress made it illegal to import any more slaves into the country.

The 1860 US census, a year before the Civil War began, recorded 3,953,760 slaves; all but 429,421 were in the deep South, which relied on labour-intensive agriculture, with cotton the most important crop. The North, on the other hand, was driven by the

JOHN BROWN

ON 16 OCTOBER 1859, the radical abolitionist John Brown led 21 men to raid the federal armoury at Harper's Ferry, Virginia (now West Virginia), hoping slaves would join him, but none did. Brown took hostages, and Colonel Robert E. Lee (the future Confederate general) was sent to end the revolt. He commanded US Marines who wounded and captured Brown, killing 10 of his followers. Brown, convicted of insurrection, treason and murder, was hanged on 2 December.

Abolitionists considered him a martyr. The song 'John Brown's Body' became popular and the words were later rewritten as 'The Battle Hymn of the Republic'.

Above: Three years before the raid, John Brown with his four sons and others had hacked to death five innocent pro-slavery men.

industrial revolution, and in this region the abolition movement grew to free all slaves. There were 11 free states and 11 slave ones in 1820, and arguments grew about which of the new territories and states would be permitted to have slaves. Congress tried several compromises but none worked.

When Abraham Lincoln was elected president in 1860, the southern states worried that his Republican Party would restrict slavery. South Carolina was the first to secede from the United States, on 20 December 1860. The following year saw 10 more leave (Mississippi, Florida, Alabama, Georgia, Louisiana, Texas, Arkansas, North Carolina, Virginia and Tennessee) to form the Confederate States.

THE CIVIL WAR

At first, it seemed the southern states could go in peace. President Lincoln said he could not remove slaves already held. 'I believe I have no lawful right to do so,' he said, 'and I have no inclination to do so'. Confederate President Jefferson Davis said, 'All we ask is to be left alone'. The *New York Tribune* advised if the southern states wanted to leave, 'we insist in letting them go in peace'.

That was not to be. When South Carolina demanded the Union's Fort Sumter on an island in Charleston harbour be handed over, Lincoln sent reinforcements instead. The war began when Confederate guns bombarded the fort on 14 April 1861. It surrendered the next day without casualties, and Lincoln called for 75,000 volunteers to put down the insurrection. Both the President and Congress said the war was being fought to preserve the Union, not to free slaves. These statements were made to keep four border states with slaves fighting on the Union side, and they did.

The war's first major battle happened on 21 July 1861 in Manassas, Virginia, near Washington, D.C. The (First) Battle of Bull Run – called the Battle of Manassas by the South – was surprisingly won by the Confederates. The Union troops fled in

Below: Politicians and society from Washington, D.C., travelled to witness the first battle at Bull Run and fled in panic when it was lost.

disarray back to Washington, suffering 2645 casualties to the Confederates' 1981.

The North, with overwhelming manpower and armaments, expected a short war and began what would become a prolonged and stalled advance on the Confederate capital in Richmond, Virginia. As battles increased during the four-year conflict, so did the deaths and injuries. Major battles occurred at Shiloh, Antietam, Fredericksburg, Chancellorsville, Gettysburg and Chickamauga. An estimated 618,222 died, the largest number of any American war. The Union lost 360,222 and the Confederacy 258,000, although recent census research estimates that the total deaths might have been 750,000.

On 22 September 1862, Lincoln issued his Emancipation Proclamation, which freed all slaves in the Confederate states. One reason for this announcement was to keep anti-slavery Britain from recognizing the Confederacy.

Most battles were in Virginia, but the two turning points happened in Gettysburg, Pennsylvania, on 3 July 1863, where General Lee suffered a devastating defeat, and Vicksburg, Mississippi, the next day, where General Grant's siege starved out the defenders, giving the Union crucial control of the Mississippi River.

The first battle of ironclad ships happened on 9 March 1862, when the Confederates' *Virginia* (previously the *Merrimack*) fought the Union's *Monitor* for three hours on the waters of Hampton Roads, Virginia, to an inconclusive

Right: General Lee (seated left) surrendered to General Grant (seated to his right) in the Virginia village of Appomattox Court House.

decision. On the high seas, the *Alabama*, built in England for the Confederacy, cruised the world with many British sailors aboard and captured 65 US merchant ships, burning 52 of them.

Lee, whose ragged army was hungry and often shoeless, surrendered to Grant on 9 April 1865. As the nation's capital celebrated, President Lincoln was assassinated on 14 April and his assailant, John Wilkes Booth, tracked down and killed. The only former Confederate executed for the war was the supervisor of the infamous Andersonville prison, where many Union prisoners died.

Congress imposed a strict military occupation during Reconstruction of the rebelling states, lasting 12 years until 1877. Those states could only rejoin the Union after 10 per cent of the population had signed an oath of loyalty to the United States.

Above: Before the war, Grant was farming near St Louis, Missouri, and surprisingly had three house slaves.

CIVIL WAR GENERALS

Among the many exceptional Civil War generals who gained victories, lost heroic battles and gave their lives, four stand above all others:

Ulysses S. Grant graduated from West Point in 1843 and fought in the Mexican War. He resigned in 1854 and took up farming and real estate, failing at both. He came into the Civil War as a colonel and two months later became a brigadier general. In February 1862, he won the Union's first victory, capturing 15,000 Confederate troops at Fort Henry, Tennessee.

Grant was known for his untidy uniform, bouts of silence and his drinking. Reporters covering his army claimed to have witnessed his spells of drunkenness.

Grant's reputation grew after conducting a six-week siege of Vicksburg, Mississippi, which he captured on 4 July 1863, taking 31,600 enemy soldiers and cutting the Confederacy in half at the Mississippi River. In March 1864, he was made general-in-chief of all four Union armies and pursued Confederate General Robert E. Lee's army through several battles, forcing his surrender on 9 April 1865 at Appomattox Court House, Virginia.

After the war, Grant was elected President of the United States in 1868 and re-elected in 1872. He published his memoirs in 1885 and 1886. 'The war has made us a nation of great power and intelligence', he wrote. 'We have but little to do to preserve peace, happiness and prosperity at home, and the respect of other nations.'

Robert E. Lee also graduated from West Point, in 1829, and fought in the Mexican War. He became superintendent at West Point in 1852, then fought Native Americans with the cavalry. In 1859, he led the US Marines who captured the radical abolitionist John Brown. President Lincoln offered him the command of the United States forces in April 1861, but Lee resigned, unable to fight against his state of Virginia, which had joined the Confederacy.

Made a brigadier general as the war began, Lee often proved superior to his outnumbered troops as he defended the Confederate capital in Richmond, Virginia. Leading the Army of Northern Virginia, he won victories at the Second Battle of Bull Run, Fredericksburg (losing 5300 casualties to the Union's 13,000) and Chancellorsville, where the enemy's army was twice his size. His decisive defeat came at Gettysburg, Pennsylvania, on 3 July 1863, and he retreated to clash with General Grant's massive army. Grant lost more men than Lee had in his army, but he still overwhelmed the Confederates and conducted a winter siege of Petersburg, Virginia, in 1864. Lee was made commander of all Confederate forces only on 6 February 1865 and two months later surrendered, ending the war. Known for his calm demeanour and kindness, Lee nevertheless said, 'It is well that war is so terrible. We should grow too fond of it'.

Lee retired to become president of Washington College (now Washington and Lee College) in Richmond. He appealed to Southerners to accept defeat and a reunited nation, saying: 'I believe it to be the duty of everyone to unite in the restoration of the country and the reestablishment of peace and harmony'.

William Tecumseh Sherman was an 1840 West Point graduate who fought in the Seminole War. He became a bank manager before becoming superintendent of a military academy in Louisiana. He joined the Union army as a colonel and was promoted to brigadier general after leading a brigade at the First Battle of Bull Run. He once talked General Grant out of retiring, and joined him in the siege of Vicksburg.

Sherman developed an emotional nervousness at times, talking to himself in a high-pitched voice. The secretary of war even sent him home in November 1861 as one newspaper ran the headline 'GENERAL

Above: Lee was known for his courteous dignity. During the war, he normally referred to the Union enemy as 'those people'.

Left: After the war, Sherman became Commander-in-Chief of the Army, a position he held from 1869 to 1884.

SHERMAN INSANE'. Sherman later wrote, 'Grant stood by me when I was crazy and I stood by him when he was drunk; and now we stand by each other always'.

Sherman became more famous by attacking Georgia. He captured Atlanta on 1 September 1864 and in November began his infamous 'march through Georgia' or 'march to the sea' vowing to 'make Georgia howl'. His soldiers took revenge on civilians, stealing provisions and burning homes. Sherman then marched to Savannah, Georgia, on the Atlantic Ocean, and up to North Carolina, where he forced a Confederate army to surrender in Raleigh four days after Lee's surrender. After peace came, he said simply, 'War is hell'.

Thomas Jonathan Jackson graduated from West Point in 1846, fought in the Mexican War, and later taught at Virginia Military Institute, taking his cadets to see the hanging of the abolitionist John Brown in 1859. Made a brigadier general when the war began, he was quickly nicknamed 'Stonewall' Jackson because his men stood firm during the First Battle of Bull Run.

Jackson was known for his eccentric habits, such as sucking lemons, laughing open-mouthed without a sound and sitting bolt upright to align his internal organs. Jackson won fame for his superb tactics, which constantly outmanoeuvred the enemy. He once defeated three Union armies in one month, putting his men on trains to reach the battles. Fighting with Lee at Chancellorsville, Jackson's own men mistook him at dusk and mortally wounded him. When his left arm was amputated, Lee lamented, 'He has lost his left arm, but I have lost my right'. Jackson died a week later.

THE MOLLY MAGUIRES
A reign of terror swept through the Pennsylvania coal fields in the 1860s and 1870s when a secret Irish group, the Molly Maguires, fought to overturn prejudices against Irish

Right: Jackson was deeply religious. He never drank, smoked or cursed and was often seen praying on and off the battlefield.

workers. Their name supposedly came from a Catholic widow in Ireland who hid in her cottage to avoid British Protestants from removing her. When the secret Irish society turned to violence in their own country, they often shouted 'Take that from a son of Molly!'

Above: On 21 June 1877, six Molly Mcquires (shown) were hanged at Pottsville, Pennsylvania, and four others at Mauch Chuck, Pennsylvania.

Many of their members went to America during the Irish Potato Famine, and some worked for the mine owners they attacked. They used intimidation and physical attacks to cripple and murder mine owners, police and other opponents. They led riots and blew up railway cars of coal. After this violence increased in 1876, the mine owners hired the famous Pinkerton detectives, who sent one of their agents, James McParland, to infiltrate the organization. His testimony indicted the leaders; 24 were convicted in 1876 and 10 hanged. Later evidence revealed that some of the trouble had been caused by agents of the mine owners.

CUSTER'S LAST STAND

Although he graduated last in his class at West Point, George Armstrong Custer became a Union general in the Civil War. He was known for his striking appearance, wearing his blond hair in ringlets and designing his own elaborate uniform. After the war, he joined the 7th US Cavalry as a lieutenant colonel in 1866 to fight the Native Americans. He won a major victory over the Cheyenne in November 1868 at the Washita River in Indian Territory (now Oklahoma).

In 1876, Custer commanded one of two columns moving against the Lakota Sioux and Cheyenne led by Sitting Bull, Crazy Horse and other chiefs, intending to force them back on their

Above: Custer and his men fight to the death at Little Big Horn. The only cavalry flag recovered from Custer's final battle was auctioned for US$32.2 million in 2010.

reservation. He arrived on the night of 24 June at their camp on the Little Bighorn River in the Montana Territory. The next morning, Custer disobeyed orders to wait for a following column and led his troops to attack the camp, dividing his force into three groups.

Outnumbered by the Native Americans, he expecting them to flee. Instead, the cavalry rode into an ambush set by several thousand warriors. The other two groups retreated and desperately fought off the attacks. Custer's men, however, were encircled. In less than an hour, all 265 men and officers were slaughtered, including two of Custer's brothers, his aide Colonel Thomas Ward Custer, and a civilian employee, Boston Custer. Two days later, the troops arrived that Custer had been ordered to wait for, and the Native Americans retreated.

SITTING BULL

At the age of 14, Sitting Bull joined his first war party and demonstrated fearlessness. He first engaged US troops in 1863 and around 1867 was made chief of the entire Sioux nation. The next year, he accepted peace with the US, giving the Sioux a reservation in the Dakota Territory (now South Dakota). When gold was discovered in the Black Hills, however, some 1000 miners rushed into land designated as the reservation. The Sioux moved into other areas and refused orders to return.

When General George Crook took men to remove them, Sitting Bull gathered Sioux, Cheyenne and Arapaho fighters. They forced the soldiers to retreat on 17 June 1876 at the Battle of the Rosebud in Montana Territory. This led to Custer's attack and slaughter at the Battle of the Little Bighorn on 25–26 June 1876. While waiting for the attack, Sitting Bull tortured himself to induce a trance in which he saw the soldiers falling from the sky like grasshoppers.

Opposite: Sitting Bull was a spiritual leader who said he received visions from *Wakan-Tanka* ('the Everywhere Spirit').

Sitting Bull led his remaining followers into Canada, but four years later famine forced his surrender. In 1885, he joined Buffalo Bill's Wild West Show and found international fame. In 1889 he became involved in the Ghost Dance movement, which believed the Native American dead would return to sweep away the white invaders. Worried about the influence of this spiritual cult, the US Army sent 43 Native American police and four Native American volunteers to Sitting Bull's house on the Grand River

BUFFALO BILL

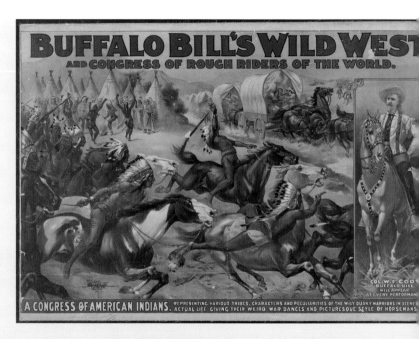

Above: Buffalo Bull's show sometimes added exotic acts to the Wild West theme.

AT THE AGE OF 14, William F(rederick) Cody joined the Pony Express that advertised for 'skinny expert riders willing to risk death daily'. He survived to join the Union army in the Civil War as a scout and cavalryman. In 1867, he earned his nickname hunting buffalo for crews building the Kansas Pacific Railroad. He claimed to have killed 4230 buffalo in 17 months. These kills and those of other pioneer hunters was a major reason Indians suffered from famine.

Cody returned to the army in 1868 to fight Native Americans, and won the Congressional Medal of Honor. He became a folk hero from real and imaginary stories in dime novels and wrote plays that he also performed in. In 1876 he again became a scout and killed Cheyenne Chief Yellow Hair in hand-to-hand combat. In 1883, Cody presented Buffalo Bill's Wild West extravaganza, starring Annie Oakley and Chief Sitting Bull, with a re-enactment of Custer's Last Stand. It was performed at Queen Victoria's Golden Jubilee in 1887 and toured Europe.

In 1890, Cody helped make peace after the massacre of some 200 Lakota at Wounded Knee, South Dakota. Cody continued to perform in his show until 1916 and died on 10 January 1917.

to arrest him on 16 December 1890. About 150 of his followers tried to rescue him. During the fight, Sitting Bull was accidentally shot and died instantly; 14 others were killed in the fighting.

CHINESE EXCLUSION ACT

Formally the Immigration Act of 1882, the law became popularly called the Chinese Exclusion Act because it barred both skilled and unskilled Chinese labourers from entering the United States. Passed by the US Congress and signed by President Chester A. Arthur, it also prohibited any who had left the country from returning. By 1870, Chinese had made up 8.6 per cent of California's population and 25 per cent of its labour force. By 1880, there were 105,465 Chinese living in the United States, with 75,000 of these in California. The year the law was passed, 39,600 people from China arrived in the United States, but three years later only 22 did.

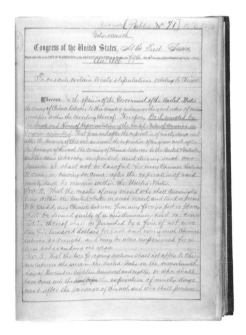

Above: The Chinese Exclusion Act was a response, mostly on the West Coast, to locals blaming unemployment on a supposed excess of Chinese workers.

This federal law was the first to exclude a specific nationality from immigrating to America. It lasted a decade and was renewed for 10 more years, with the additional requirement for Chinese to carry identification or be deported. The law was made permanent in 1904 and was only repealed in 1943 when the United States and China became allies in World War II.

THE SPANISH–AMERICAN WAR

Cuba began seeking independence from Spain in 1895, but any hint of rebellion was brutally suppressed by the Spanish. This created American public support for the Cuban cause. Among those reporting the early tension from Cuba was Lieutenant Winston Churchill, a correspondent for *The Daily Graphic*, although his official cover was as a military observer with the Spanish forces.

When the USS *Maine* battleship was sent to rescue Americans from rioting, it sank on 15 February 1898 in Havana Harbour from a mysterious explosion, killing 260 sailors. Sensational

THE 'ROUGH RIDERS' INCLUDED MANY TYPES, FROM COLLEGE BOYS TO GAMBLERS AND PROSPECTORS.

American newspapers like the *New York World* and *New York Journal* whipped up public sentiment for a war. The *Journal's* owner and editor, William Randolph Hearst, was even credited with starting the war, having cabled his illustrator, Frederic Remington, saying 'You furnish the pictures and I'll furnish the war'.

Although Spain began a program to grant limited self-government to Cuba, the US Congress passed a resolution granting the president's use of force if needed. Spain declared war on the United States on 24 April 1898; the US responded with its war declaration the following day. On 1 May, a US naval squadron under Commodore George Dewey sailed to the Philippines and destroyed the Spanish fleet in Manila Bay. By August, Manila was occupied by US troops.

In Cuba, an American force under General William Shafter landed near Santiago. Among the soldiers was Lieutenant Colonel Theodore Roosevelt and his 1st Volunteer Cavalry, popularly known as the 'Rough Riders'. The overall troops advanced to Santiago to force the Spanish Caribbean Fleet, commanded by Admiral Pascual Cervera y Topete, out of

Below: Colonel Theodore Roosevelt poses (wearing braces) with his Rough Riders cavalry. They included 1060 men with 1258 horses and mules.

THEODORE ROOSEVELT

BEFORE HE FOUGHT IN the Spanish–American War, Theodore Roosevelt had graduated from Harvard University and served as New York City's police commissioner from 1895 until 1897. He was the assistant secretary of the Navy when war broke out, and resigned to organize the 1st Volunteer Cavalry that he led during the war.

These 'Rough Riders' included many types, from college boys to gamblers and prospectors. Fighting in Cuba, they made famous charges up Kettle Hill and San Juan Hill on 1 July 1898, clearing out the Spanish. They lost a third of their men, the war's highest casualty rate of any US unit.

The war made Roosevelt a hero. The year it ended, he was elected governor of New York and in 1901 US Vice President. When President William McKinley was assassinated that year, Roosevelt became the nation's youngest ever president, at 42. He was re-elected in 1905. He initiated construction of the Panama Canal and

Above: President Roosevelt often quoted a West African saying for his foreign policy: 'Speak softly and carry a big stick'.

mediated peace between Japan and Russia, earning him the Nobel Peace Prize.

Roosevelt's nickname of 'Teddy' for Theodore was used for the soft toy teddy bear after the president went hunting in Mississippi and refused to shoot a black bear (an old one, not a cub).

the city's harbour. It sailed off along the coast on 3 July and was destroyed by American guns.

The one-sided war, which cost America only 400 battle deaths, ended on 10 December 1898 by the Treaty of Paris. Spain renounced its claim to Cuba, ceded Puerto Rico and Guam to the United States, and transferred sovereignty over the Philippines for $20 million. The US strongly denied that it was building a colonial empire, but took pride in the new distant possessions and its growing international reputation and power.

7

GOTHIC LIVES

The Victorians were fascinated by people who were unusual or dangerous, often in a strange and grotesque way. This interest was fuelled by novels about monsters and horror, and also by real people such as the Elephant Man and Jack the Ripper.

ALL SOCIETIES are intrigued by and fear the abnormal, but this was amplified in Victorian times by popular newspapers that highlighted murders and other crimes with sensational headlines, such as 'Murder and Mutilation in Whitechapel' and 'Hideous Mutilation of Body and Face'.

In addition, the popular novels about Dracula and Frankenstein had some readers believing in the existence of vampires and monsters. Freak shows and travelling circuses were another major appeal, displaying everyone from Siamese twins to bearded ladies, and many Victorians could recall the organized tours to view and laugh at the mentally ill 'freaks' in the Bedlam Hospital.

Opposite: An image that seeks to capture the horror of Edgar Allan Poe's novel *The Fall of the House of Usher.*

FRANKENSTEIN

The English author Mary Shelley published her novel about the monster created by Doctor Frankenstein in 1818. The Gothic story *Frankenstein; or, The Modern Prometheus* became an instant success among nineteenth-century readers fascinated by its combination of science and horror. Her book has been

described as one of the first works of science fiction. The danger of creating life in a laboratory has remained a fascinating subject since the Victorian era, inspiring numerous books and films about manmade monsters even more vicious than Frankenstein's confused and frightened creation.

Mary Wollstonecraft Godwin was born on 30 August 1797 in London. In 1814, she ran off to France with the young poet Percy Bysshe Shelley; they married in 1816 after his first wife committed suicide. The idea for the book came that year when they joined Lord Byron, his physician, John Polidori (who later wrote *The Vampyre*), and others in Geneva. During one night of thunder and lightning as they gathered in the candlelit house of Villa Diodati, Mary listened to their discussions about the

Above: Apart from *Frankenstein*, Mary Shelley wrote several other novels, including *The Last Man* (1826), about a plague destroying the human race.

spark of life and Byron's suggestion for a contest to write ghost stories. When she went to bed, she closed her eyes and imagined a scientist kneeling 'beside the thing he had put together' that began to 'show signs of life and stir with an uneasy, half-vital motion'. At that time, she recalled, 'Frankenstein the monster and *Frankenstein* the book had both been born'.

After her husband's death in 1822, Mary Shelley returned to London and had a successful writing career, including novels, biographies and travel books. She died on 1 February 1851.

MADAME TUSSAUD

Marie Tussaud was born in 1761 as Marie Grosholtz in Strasbourg, France. She was taught wax modelling by a physician. By 1780, she had become an art tutor to a sister of King Louis XVI and lived at the royal court in Versailles. After the French Revolution in 1789, she was imprisoned with her mother, but won her freedom by making death masks of the freshly decapitated king, queen and other nobles. She inherited the doctor's wax exhibition in 1794 and the following year married François Tussaud.

Tussaud left her husband in 1802 (she never saw him again), and travelled with her two sons to put her exhibition on display in London's Lyceum Theatre. She was unable to return to France due to the Napoleonic Wars, and subsequently toured her waxworks around Britain and Ireland for the next 33 years. She established a base in London in 1835 at the Baker Street Bazaar with the separate room that became the Chamber of Horrors. The exhibition contained some 400 wax figures of victims of the French Revolution and other famous people, including George III and Benjamin Franklin. Tussaud died in 1850, and in 1884 her grandsons moved the exhibit to its present site on Marylebone Road in London. Today there are ten Madame Tussauds exhibitions around the world, including four in America.

THE SIAMESE TWINS

The conjoined twins, Chang and Eng, were born in Siam (now Thailand) in 1811, and the term 'Siamese' is still colloquially used to describe conjoined twins. Chang and Eng were connected by a band several inches long at their midsections. A travelling British merchant realized their commercial value and convinced them to move to the United States when they were 18. Arriving in Boston, they were exhibited as the 'Siamese Double Boys'. They became famous as freaks, exhibiting themselves in a show that included them turning somersaults and back flips. They went to London in 1830 and the next year toured Europe.

Below: Even Madam Tussaud became a wax figure. She had her own portrait rendered in wax eight years before she died.

CHAMBER OF HORRORS

WHEN MARIE TUSSAUD OPENED a permanent exhibition of waxworks in London in 1835, she set aside a room for gruesome exhibits of the French Revolution, charging sixpence to enter. In 1846, *Punch* magazine coined the name 'Chamber of Horrors' for this room. Crowds packed the room to pore over the display, which included the heads of the guillotined Louis XVI and Marie Antoinette, Madame du Barry (Louis XVI's mistress) and Robespierre, among others. A model of a guillotine was also exhibited.

Tussaud added exhibits of murderers and other criminals who had been hanged. By 1886, these included Arthur Thistlewood, who in 1820 had planned to murder the British cabinet; William Burke and William Hare, who killed 16 people in 1828 in Edinburgh, Scotland, to sell the corpses to a doctor for dissection; Marie Manning, who with her husband murdered her lover in 1849; and the serial poisoner Mary Ann Cotton, who was hanged in 1783.

In 2016, the Chamber of Horrors closed until further notice after families complained that it was too traumatic for young children. Recent innovations at Madame Tussauds had included people in costume jumping out and screaming at the passing crowd.

Below: The heads of King Louis XVI and Marie Antoinette were quite possibly made from their death masks.

After a decade of exhibitions, Eng and Chang retired with ample money, buying land in North Carolina as well as dozens of slaves. They became US citizens, borrowing the surname Bunker from the man standing behind them at the naturalization office. They were married in 1843 to the sisters Sarah and Adelaide Yates, who talked them out of going through a planned operation to separate them. The marriage prompted a shocked and violent public reaction. Men smashed the windows of the house of the sisters' father and threatened to burn his crops. One newspaper called the marriage 'bestial' and another wondered if the wives should be indicted for wedding 'a quadruped'. Nevertheless, the marriage proved loving, with both women giving birth in 1844. The couples went on to have 21 children (11 by Eng and 10 by Chang).

Running short on money, the twins returned to touring. In Britain, some newspapers declared it was 'disgusting' to see these 'human monsters' as husbands and fathers. Chang suffered a stroke in 1870 that paralyzed his right side and he began drinking heavily. He died on 17 January 1874. His brother said simply, 'Then I am going' and died two and a half hours later.

Above: When Chang and Eng planned to visit France in 1831, French authorities banned the visit, worried they would upset women.

EDGAR ALLAN POE

An American writer known for his short stories and poetry of fear and horror, Poe was born on 19 January 1809 in Boston, Massachusetts. His macabre short stories include *The Fall of the House of Usher* (1839) and *The Premature Burial* (1844). His 1841 work *The Murders in the Rue Morgue* is considered the first modern detective story, while *The Raven* (1845) won national acclaim and remains a popular poem.

Poe's life was filled with fame and failures. His studies at the University of Virginia ended in 1826 because of his gambling. He joined the army under the name of Edgar A. Perry. His guardian secured an appointment to the US Military Academy at West Point, but Poe missed a week of classes and drills in order to be expelled, which he was.

Above: Poe had a drinking problem and went on public sprees. This led to the belief that he was a drug addict.

Opposite: When Barnum died, the *Washington Post* called him 'the most widely known American that ever lived'.

Poe went to New York City and published a volume of poems, then to Richmond, Virginia, in 1835 to edit the *Southern Literary Messenger* and marry his 13-year-old cousin, Virginia Clemm. He was fired from his Richmond job for drinking and in 1839 ended up in Philadelphia to co-edit *Burton's Gentleman's Magazine* and publish his supernatural horror story, *The Fall of the House of Usher*. In 1842 he wrote *The Masque of the Red Death* and in 1844 was co-editor of the *New York Mirror*.

By 1849, Poe had intimations of his death as he travelled from Richmond to Baltimore, Maryland. Nearly a week later, on 3 October 1849, he was found lying in a gutter outside a polling station, delirious and dressed in shabby second-hand clothes. For four days, he had fits of delirium and hallucinations, finally dying on 7 October. The night before his death, he repeatedly called out for 'Reynolds' – a name that remains a mystery.

Poe's death was officially listed as swelling of the brain, but his dying is so mysterious that the magazine of the Smithsonian Institute listed nine possibilities: alcohol, influenza, murder, brain tumour, rabies, beaten by a ruffian, attacked after being forced to vote for a candidate, carbon monoxide poisoning from indoor lighting, and heavy mercury poisoning from a doctor's prescription.

P.T. BARNUM

Although P.T. Barnum is remembered as part founder of Ringling Bros. and Barnum & Bailey Circus, he did not join that enterprise until his sixties. Before that, he made his name by presenting 'wonders' (often freaks) in his American Museum in New York City. Among his exhibited curiosities were the Siamese Twins, Eng and Chang; tiny Charles Stratton, whom Barnum renamed General Tom Thumb; Josephine Clofullia, a Swiss bearded lady; and the Feejee (Fiji) Mermaid, whose orangutan head on a fish body turned out to be faked.

Phineas Taylor Barnum was born on 5 July 1810 in Bethel, Connecticut. He moved to New York in 1834 and the next year pulled off his first successful hoax on the public by presenting an elderly African American woman as the 161-year-old nurse of George Washington. In 1842, he bought the American Museum and added to its exhibits of waxworks and stuffed animals with live freaks and spectacular entertainments. Among its 82 million visitors, attracted by his overblown publicity, were Charles Dickens and the Prince of Wales, the future Edward VII. Barnum sold the museum in 1868 after two fires had damaged it.

One of his great successes in real entertainment was bringing the famous Swedish soprano Jenny Lind to America, calling her the Swedish Nightingale. Her first concert in 1850 in New York drew 5000 people, with more gathered outside.

When Barnum entered the three-ring circus business in 1880, he was quick to advertise it as 'The Greatest Show on Earth' and added the

Below: Barnum presented four-year-old Charles Stratton as being the age of 11 to increase the wonder of his size.

huge elephant Jumbo, whose name is still used as an epithet for anything large. He also continued the tradition of a sideshow of freaks.

Barnum became seriously ill when 81 and had a New York newspaper publish his obituary in advance so he could relish his accomplishments. He died on 7 April 1891 in Bridgeport, Connecticut, where he had been mayor. Throughout his life, Barnum had relished his image as a deceptive promoter, calling himself the 'Prince of Humbugs'. The quote 'There's a sucker born every minute' continues to be attributed to him without proof.

TOM THUMB

In 1842, Barnum was introduced to Charles Sherwood Stratton, a four-year-old boy who weighed only 6.8kg (15lb) and stood 66cm (2ft 2in) high. Recognizing his financial value, Barnum hired Charles and billed him as 'General Tom Thumb, Man in Miniature', saying he was 11 and recently arrived from England.

Audiences were amazed at the miniature dwarf, whom Barnum added to the Hall of Living Curiosities at his museum. Barnum took him to England, where Tom was granted an audience with Queen Victoria. He sang several cheeky songs and did impressions. As he was leaving, a spaniel began barking and Tom took out a tiny sword and pretended to battle the dog, bringing laughter from the queen and her court. She then granted him a second audience.

EVENTUALLY TOM THUMB, WHO HAD GROWN TO 99CM (3FT 3IN), WAS SEEN BY 50 MILLION PEOPLE ACROSS EUROPE.

Barnum and Tom Thumb continued to tour through Europe, appearing in costumed dramas before enthusiastic crowds in France, Germany and Belgium. Eventually Tom, who had grown to 99cm (3ft 3in), was seen by 50 million people.

In 1863, Barnum arranged for Charles to marry another of his small people, Lavinia Warren. The wedding was covered on the front page of the *New York Times* and other newspapers, and President Lincoln hosted a party for the couple after the

JUMBO

In 1880, P.T. Barnum saw a gigantic seven-ton African elephant at London's zoo and two years later purchased him for $10,000. The 20-year-old animal had arrived in 1865 from a menagerie in Paris. The name Jumbo was a combination of two Swahili words, *jambo* (hello) and *jumbe* (chief). Queen Victoria protested in vain about the sale of what she regarded as a national treasure. Ten horses were needed to haul his crate to a London dock for his voyage to New York, where he arrived on 9 April 1882. Jumbo, who stood 3.5m (11ft 6in) tall, was displayed at the Hippodrome (later Madison Square Garden) and then joined Barnum's circus tours in his own railway carriage. He was viewed by some 20 million people in three years.

On 15 September 1885, Jumbo was hit and killed by an express train in the Canadian town of St Thomas, Ontario. One story said he saved a smaller elephant, shoving it away before being hit. Barnum had Jumbo's body stuffed and displayed by the circus for two years before donating it to a Boston museum, where it was destroyed by fire in 1975. The skeleton remains at the New York's American Museum of Natural History.

Below: After Jumbo's death, Barnum took his skeleton standing 4 metres (13ft) on an international tour.

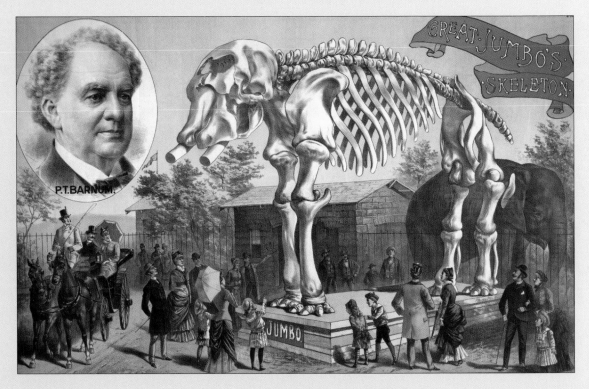

ceremony. Barnum hired different babies to be presented as their child, but said it had died when he tired of the deception. The couple settled down in Charles' hometown of Bridgeport, Connecticut, in a house with small furniture. Charles died suddenly in 1883 at the age of 45.

THE ELEPHANT MAN

Joseph Merrick was a man who was badly deformed from an unknown disease that increased the circumference of his head to nearly 1m (3ft) and caused a distortion of his jaw, making speech difficult. His right arm and leg also increased in size and his hip was deformed, forcing him to walk with a cane. The back of his head had a growth of spongy skin.

Merrick was born on 5 August 1862 in Leicester, England. He looked normal until the age of five, when the abnormal bone and skin growths began. He was confined to a workhouse when 17 but ran away after four years, in 1883, to join a freak show. A London physician, Frederick Treves, saw him on exhibition in a London shop and had him admitted for treatment into London Hospital in 1886. Treves' interest drew the attention of London's society, who made visits to view the 'Elephant Man', as he was then known. At the age of 27, Merrick died accidentally on 11 April 1890 from suffocation due to the weight of his head.

Merrick's skeleton is now kept in a private room at the medical school of Queen Mary University of London.

Above: Joseph Merrick's sad, fascinating life was made into a play, *The Elephant Man*, in 1977 and a film in 1980.

DR JEKYLL AND MR HYDE

Robert Louis Stevenson shocked Victorian readers with his 1886 novella, *The Strange Case of Dr Jekyll and Mr Hyde*. It suggested

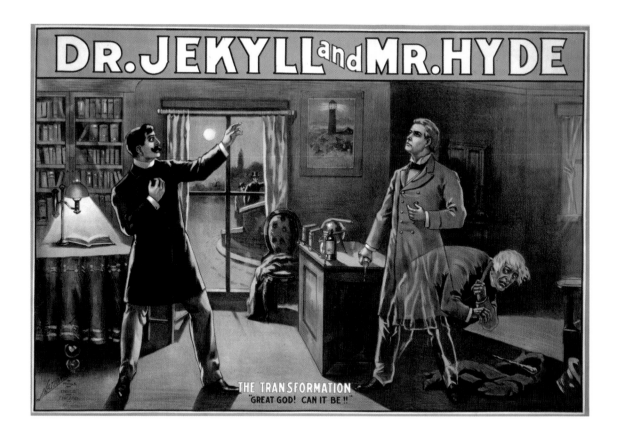

DR. JEKYLL and MR. HYDE

THE TRANSFORMATION
"GREAT GOD! CAN IT BE!!"

Above: A poster from the late 1880s emphasized Dr Jekyll's frightening transformation from Victorian decency to pure evil.

the evil that exists within normal people and that Victorian respectability might be a cover for depravity or at least depraved thoughts. The plot also played on stories of monsters created by laboratory scientists. Dr Henry Jekyll is a respectable man who discovers a serum to transform himself into the murderous Edward Hyde. Jekyll struggles hopelessly against his addiction to become Hyde, but the changes begin to happen spontaneously. He discovers another serum to reverse the transformation, but the drink begins to fail and Jekyll, realizing that he will forever be Hyde, commits suicide.

FARINI EXHIBITED KRAO IN 1883 IN AMERICAN MUSEUMS, AND SHE BECAME ADEPT AT CREATING HER STORY OF LIVING WITH MONKEY-LIKE PEOPLE WHO LIVED IN TREES.

Stevenson was born on 13 November 1850 in Edinburgh, Scotland. He studied law at Edinburgh University and graduated in 1875, but never practised. He travelled to France and wrote travel books. In 1877, Stevenson began to write short stories, including an Arabian series of grotesque romances. He went to California in 1879 to be with an American woman, Fanny Osbourne. She had been previously married but had separated from her unfaithful husband, and married Stevenson in 1880.

Suffering from tuberculosis, Stevenson wrote his best-known novels – *Treasure Island*, published in 1883, and *Kidnapped* in 1886 – the same year as his Jekyll and Hyde story. The latter, the idea for which had come to him in a dream, made his name to many readers, as he found out the following year when visiting America. Beginning in 1888, Stevenson spent the remainder of his years wandering around the South Sea Islands. He died on 3 December 1894 and was buried on top of Mount Vaea in Samoa, where he had a home.

THE GREAT FARINI

Known as Canada's greatest showman and promoter, William Leonard Hunt took the name of Signor Guillermo Antonio

'THE MISSING LINK'

KRAO, a Laotian girl whose body was covered by coarse black hair, arrived in London in 1882. Victorians were still debating Charles Darwin's 1859 theory of evolution, and Krao was advertised as 'the Missing Link' between apes and humankind. Krao was exhibited at the Royal Aquarium in London by the Canadian promoter William Hunt, the Great Farini. Having funded the expedition that discovered her, he eventually adopted her.

Farini exhibited Krao in 1883 in American museums, and she became adept at creating her story of living with monkey-like people who lived in trees.

American newspapers doubted her story because of her intelligence. In 1885, she toured as a freak with a small Midwestern circus, earning $200 a week, and was then displayed in a New York museum. The public were told that she kept food in her cheek pouches, had 13 ribs like an ape, and had an extra backbone like a gorilla. She moved to Brooklyn and worked as the bearded lady at Coney Island. She wore a veil when out on the city streets. Krao died on 16 April 1926. She had asked to be cremated so her body could not be exhibited. New York law prevented this, and she was properly buried.

IN 1876, FARINI INVENTED THE DEVICE USED FOR HIS NEW 'HUMAN CANNONBALL' ACT.

Farini and billed himself as the Great Farini. Born on 10 June 1838 in Lockport, New York, to Canadian parents, he moved with his family in 1843 to Hope Township in Ontario, Canada. He later trained as a tightrope walker and in 1860 amazed an audience by walking across Niagara Falls in a sack and then carrying a man on his back. By 1866, he had become a sensation in London and Europe with the Flying Farinis trapeze artists. His featured partner was his adopted son, whom he billed as a girl called Lulu, 'The Eighth Wonder of the World'.

After serving with the Union Army in the Civil War, Farini performed in Havana, Cuba, with his first wife, before 30,000 spectators. As he carried her on his back, she waved to the crowd and lost her balance. He grabbed her skirt but it ripped and she fell to her death.

Below: Farini's 'Missing Link', Krao, was born in Laos with excessive hair growth. He said she proved Darwin's theory of evolution.

In 1876, Farini invented the device used for his new 'human cannonball' act. Farini began displaying freaks and entertainments in 1882 at London's Royal Aquarium. Among his exhibits were Krao, billed as the 'Missing Link', and the tattooed Captain George Costentenus. Farini also worked with the American showman P.T. Barnum. In 1885, Farini walked across Africa's Kalahari Desert and claimed to be the first white man to accomplish that feat and to have discovered the ruined Lost City of the Kalahari.

In 1886, Farini married his third wife,

a German concert pianist. They lived in England, Canada, the United States and Germany, where he produced a 30-volume history of World War I. Farini was also a renowned botanist and painter. He died at the age of 90 on 17 January 1929 in Port Hope, Ontario.

THE TIME MACHINE

H.G. Wells' 1895 novel *The Time Machine* provided Victorians with one of the earliest examples of science fiction. Its plot involved a nameless Victorian scientist who makes a time machine that sends him into the future, the year 802,701, where he encounters the Eloi, a meek and indolent people whose needs, such as food and clothing, are taken care of by the Morlocks, who live underground. Before he returns to his own time, the scientist discovers that the Morlocks also kill and eat the Eloi. Some critics believe that Wells was making a statement refuting Darwin's idea of evolution providing a better world.

Herbert George Wells was born on 21 September 1866 in Bromley, Kent. He graduated from London University in 1888 and became a science teacher. After a failed marriage to a cousin, he ran away with a former student, whom he married in 1895. *The Time Machine* was Wells' first novel and an overnight success.

Below: A book cover for H.G. Wells' novel used an artist's impression of how his fantastic time machine would look.

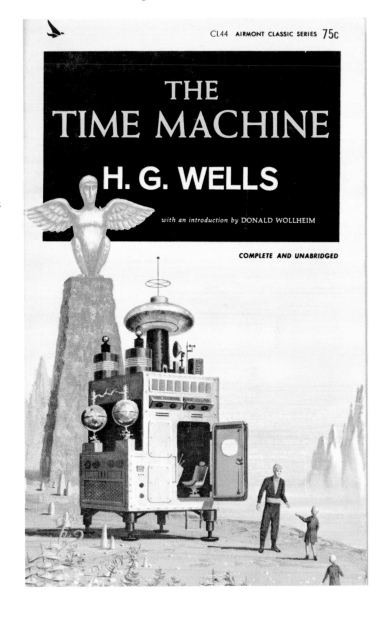

CL44   AIRMONT CLASSIC SERIES   75c

THE TIME MACHINE
H. G. WELLS

with an introduction by DONALD WOLLHEIM

COMPLETE AND UNABRIDGED

Among his other scientific novels were *The Invisible Man* (1897), *The War of the Worlds* (1898), *Tales of Space and Time* (1899), *The First Men in the Moon* (1901) and *The Island of Doctor Moreau* (1906). The latter story involved experiments that created half-human creatures called Beast Folk.

Wells was a visionary who foresaw global warming, germ warfare, laser beams, radio, television, and many other modern devices. A socialist, he spent much of his latter years promoting equality and human rights issues. His work *The Rights of Man* (1940), about fundamental freedoms, was so influential that many of its points were written into the Universal Declaration of Human Rights that was adopted by the United Nations in 1948. Wells died on 13 August 1946 in London; his ashes were scattered at sea.

Below: Clemence Houseman, here with her playwright brother Laurence Houseman, was an activist in the women's suffrage movement.

THE WERE-WOLF

Considered the classic werewolf tale of the late nineteenth century, Clemence Housman's short story *The Were-Wolf* was published in 1896. The plot involves a beautiful woman named White Fell who is actually a werewolf that kills villagers. Christian is the only villager who can see White Fell in her murderous werewolf form; his brother, Sweyn, is enamoured of the woman. Ultimately, the aptly named Christian sacrifices himself to save Sweyn from becoming the werewolf's next victim.

DRACULA

Bram Stoker's gothic horror novel took seven years to write. It was published in 1897 and introduced the character Count Dracula. Earlier vampire stories had been written, such as John Polidori's *Vampyre* in 1819, but Stoker's Transylvanian character appealed to the Victorians' sense of masculine dominance and inhibited sex. It would provide the model for a multitude of vampire stories and films that are still popular today.

Stoker, an Irish writer, had first written the story as a play, *The Un-Dead*. He worked as the business manager for London's Lyceum Theatre from 1878 to 1898, and based his character on the fluid movements and mincing gestures of the actor Henry Irving. He hoped Irving would play the title role, but the actor refused and said he never wanted to see it again, prompting Stoker to do more research for a book. The story itself was based on Vlad Tepes, better known as 'Vlad the Impaler', a fifteenth-century Romanian prince known for his cruelty and his habit of impaling enemies on stakes. While following the legends of vampires, Stoker added his own idea of Dracula being able to transform into a bat.

Stoker said his book was a combination of mystery and fact. 'A person may have fallen into a death-like trance and been buried before the time,' he noted. 'Afterwards the body may have been dug up and found alive, and from this, a horror seized upon the people, and in their ignorance they imagined that a vampire was about'.

Above: A poster for Francis Ford Coppola's 1992 film, *Dracula*, in which the vampire is more motivated by romance than bloodlust.

8

SCIENCE AND TECHNOLOGY

Victorians were convinced that they had created the modern world. An explosion of scientific discoveries and inventions came along just as the Industrial Revolution began to mass-produce and distribute the latest consumer products. With great pride, Queen Victoria said that 'every conceivable invention' could be found in London's 1851 Great Exhibition.

THE MOST visible changes came in transportation, with Victorians being the first to experience railways, the Underground, motor cars and even bicycles. Equally amazing were communication advances, with the advent of electricity, radio waves, the telegraph and the telephone. Entertainment that had only been available in the form of live stage performances could now be recorded by the phonograph and with film that even displayed moving pictures. Of more importance than any of these was the arrival of modern medicine. The discovery of germs quickly led to the use of antiseptics during surgery and the practices of sterilization and pasteurization.

Opposite: Queen Victoria and Prince Albert at the extravagant opening of the Great Exhibition on 1 May 1851.

THE STEAMBOAT

Americans led the way in developing the steamboat in order to speed transportation along the Mississippi River. Robert Fulton had the first success with a single-cylinder steam engine fuelled by oak and pinewood that powered two side paddle wheels. In 1807, he had a trial run of 240km (150 miles) on the Hudson River from New York City to Albany in New York State. He made the distance in 32 hours, compared to the four days taken by sailing sloops. That same year, Fulton began the first commercial steamboat trips on the Hudson with the *Clermont*.

In 1811, Fulton designed the *New Orleans*, built in Pittsburgh, Pennsylvania, and he and his partner Robert Livingston took it to the city of New Orleans. However, the steamboat was unable to make the return trip upstream any further than Natchez, Mississippi, the same fate befalling three other steamboats that Fulton built in New Orleans.

During the War of 1812 against Britain, Fulton devised the first steam warship to protect New York from the British fleet. The *Fulton* was launched in 1814, carrying heavy guns and armour. It never went to battle, however, peace being declared months later.

Below: Fulton's *Clermont* was built in New York City by Charles Brown. Its full name was *North River Steamboat of Clermont*.

ROBERT FULTON

THE SON OF IRISH immigrants in Pennsylvania, Robert Fulton attended a Quaker school and became an apprentice in a Philadelphia jewellery shop. Before his success with steamboats, Fulton had had many grand ideas that failed.

Fulton took up painting and moved to London in 1787, where his artistic skills were not appreciated. He became interested in canal engineering while there, but none of his canal designs were accepted. In 1797, Fulton moved to Paris, intent on selling his idea of a submarine, the *Nautilus*. When the French government rejected it, Fulton financed the construction himself. The government approved an attack on British ships, but the *Nautilus* proved too slow. In 1804, back in London, the government liked his submarine, but his two raids against French ships failed. Two years later in New York, he gained the interest of the US government, but the trial was another disaster.

Fulton's frustrating travels did eventually start him on the path that would make his name. In 1801 in Paris, he met Robert Livingston, who had a steamship monopoly in New York State. The two men built a steamship in Paris, with limited success, and collected parts for the engine that would be used for the successful trial in America in 1807.

Above: Five years after Fulton's success with the *Clermont*, he was running steamboat services on six rivers and the Chesapeake Bay.

Fulton's monopoly on the Mississippi River was broken in 1816 by Henry Miller Shreve, who launched the *Washington* for trips between New Orleans and Louisville, Kentucky. Shreve redesigned his steamship to take shallow waters and used a high-pressure steam engine to travel upstream. He also added an upper deck that became the familiar profile of all later Mississippi steamboats. Shreve would found the town of Shreveport, Louisiana, in 1837.

ISAMBARD KINGDOM BRUNEL

BORN IN 1806 IN Portsmouth, Brunel was the son of a French engineer and studied in Paris when 14. In 1831, he designed the Clifton Suspension Bridge, still the symbol of Bristol. Its span was then the longest in the world. He later worked with his father, Marc, in designing the Thames Tunnel, which opened in 1843.

Brunel's greatest accomplishment was as chief engineer for the Great Western Railway in 1833. His choice of a broader gauge created a smoother and faster journey. He used innovative works to smooth the railway's long line from London to Bristol, which included bridges, tunnels and viaducts. His impressive skills were next used to design docks, such as those at Bristol, Cardiff and Milford Haven, and three of the world's most impressive ships. Brunel's *Great Western*, launched in 1837, was the largest steamship of its time and the first offering a transatlantic service, going from Bristol to New York. The *Great Britain* in 1843 was the world's first iron-hulled passenger liner driven by a screw propeller and steam, the prototype of modern ships. Brunel also co-designed the largest ship then built, the *Great Eastern*, nicknamed the 'Leviathan'. It was launched in 1859 – also the year Brunel died.

Left: Brunel's Clifton Suspension Bridge ran into financial difficulties. It remained unfinished three decades later when he died.

Besides transporting cotton, sugar and other goods, steamboats evolved into luxurious pleasure boats offering passengers ornate rooms along with entertainment and gambling. Captains of two rival steamboats would often engage in races for the enjoyment of passengers. This golden age of the steamboat ended in the 1870s when railroads expanded across the country, offering fast transportation to towns not connected to the river.

RAILWAYS

Trains opened up long-range mass transportation to the Victorians and created the new idea of suburbs. The world's first successful run on tracks by a steam locomotive occurred in 1804 at ironworks in South Wales. It was designed and built by the British mechanical engineer Richard Trevithick.

The first regular passenger service began in the United States in 1827 with the Baltimore & Ohio Railroad. British rail travel started in 1830, running 10km (6 miles) from Canterbury to Whitstable. A major line began that year between Liverpool and Manchester, although a member of parliament was run down and killed during the opening ceremony, in what was the first railway accident.

Below: Richard Trevithick's locomotive made its first historic trip covering nine miles while carrying 10 tonnes of iron in five wagons.

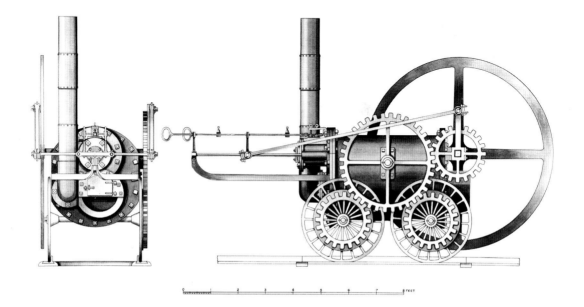

By 1847, Britain had 576 railway companies and more than 14,000km (8700 miles) of new track. The growth of rail travel in Britain was hindered by the tracks having different gauges.

THE IDEA OF A SELF-PROPELLED VEHICLE GOES AS FAR BACK AS LEONARDO DA VINCI IN THE FIFTEENTH CENTURY.

In 1844, standard gauges were introduced so the national railway system would have interchangeable tracks. One gauge that never changed was the broad one chosen in 1833 by the exceptional engineer Isambard Kingdom Brunel for the Great Western Railway connecting London and Bristol.

A lesser but still irritating problem was the lack of a standard time at different stations. Local time in effect created different time zones within a few miles. Passengers from London to Oxford, for example, would have to set their watches back five minutes. This confusion ended with the adoption of London's Greenwich Mean Time for every station, first in 1840 by the Great Western Railway. Nearly all the other stations had switched to 'railway time' by 1855.

Other nations were not far behind in establishing rail travel. Canada's first line opened in 1836, connecting St Lawrence and Lake Champlain, after trial runs were made at night so the public would not be frightened. The first passenger train in India came into service in 1853 between Bombay and Thane. Australia's rail service began the following year between Melbourne and Port Melbourne. China's first train, built by the British, went into operation in 1876 between Shanghai and Woosung.

THE MOTOR CAR

The idea of a self-propelled vehicle goes as far back as Leonardo da Vinci in the fifteenth century. Inventors in the eighteenth century tried various fuels, including air, steam and coal gas. Steam buses appeared on Paris streets at the beginning of the nineteenth century, and steam carriages were tried out in Britain in the 1830s. They were noisy and smoky as well as dangerous. America had success with the Stanley Steamer, introduced in 1896. The country's first electric car was built in 1890 by William Morrison, despite an absence of ways to charge the battery.

In 1858, the Belgium engineer Jean Lenoir built the first commercially successful internal combustion engine. Experiments with gasoline-powered cars were conducted in the 1860s in France and Austria, but it was two Germans who made an impact. Karl Benz produced his first three-wheel car in 1885 and ten years later had sold 1132 of his four-wheel Viktoria and Velo models. Gottlieb Daimler's version followed the next year; this had the engine in the rear, providing four speeds and a belt that drove the four wheels. The two firms that were established by their work merged in 1926 as Daimler-Benz and began selling the prestigious Mercedes-Benz brand.

Above: Charles Duryea poses in his gasoline-powered car. He and his brother, Frank, argued over who had developed the car.

Britain entered serious car production in 1891 after Frederick Simms, a London engineer, acquired the rights to Daimler's engine. He sold them to H.J. Lawson, who formed the Daimler Motor Company in 1896 and began manufacturing the cars in Coventry.

The first successful American gasoline car was built in 1893 by the brothers Charles and Frank Duryea in Springfield, Massachusetts. By 1898, the United States had more than 100 companies established to produce automobiles. The Oldsmobile, built by Ransom Eli Olds in 1899, became the first commercially successful American-made automobile in 1904. It would be four more years before Henry Ford mass-produced his first Model T, a sturdy and cheap car that became the nation's favourite.

Above: The earliest reliably dated photograph of people was taken by Daguerre on an early spring morning in 1838 in Paris.

PHOTOGRAPHY

Centuries before the camera was invented, the camera obscura was used to capture images. This was a dark room or a box with a hole in one wall that threw an image on the opposite wall where it could be sketched. A lens was added in the late sixteenth century, but the goal remained to capture the real image on paper.

Joseph Niépce, an amateur French inventor, took the first photographic image in 1826. He fitted a camera obscura with a pewter plate to capture a picture of his country courtyard from a window using the sun for his heliographic process. The exposure time was eight hours. Also that year, he copied a portrait of

MATHEW B. BRADY

BORN IN NEW YORK State, Brady moved to New York City to produce jewellery cases, but became intrigued by the new daguerreotype process. In 1844, he opened a portrait studio in the city and in 1849 another one in Washington, DC. In 1855, he switched to the wet-plate process and opened his National Photographic Art Gallery on Pennsylvania Avenue in Washington. It attracted the rich and famous, including more than one visit from President Abraham Lincoln. At the same time, Brady and his assistant Alexander Gardner turned out small, inexpensive prints called carte-de-visite photographs that were bought by families, especially those who had sons in the Civil War.

When the war began, the Union army allowed Brady to follow and photograph the action. He did this in dangerous conditions while carrying his equipment and chemicals in a covered wagon that could be made dark to develop his glass negatives. Bemused soldiers nicknamed the wagon 'the Whatisit'. Because Brady had failing eyesight, his assistants, Gardner and Timothy O'Sullivan, took most of the photographs. They produced more than 3500 showing camp life and the aftermath of battles with dead bodies strewn over the ground. Brady exhibited these pictures as 'The Dead of Antietam' at his New York studio in September 1862 during the war. The graphic views of this first photographed war, of the dead, dying and wounded, shocked the public, and some urged that the war be discontinued. When peace returned, Brady filed for bankruptcy in 1873. He sold his entire wartime portfolio to the US government for $25,000, and it is now an invaluable collection in the Library of Congress.

Above: Brady (above) photographed Confederate General Robert E. Lee after the war on the back porch of his Richmond home.

Cardinal d'Amboise for three hours and etched the pewter plate so prints could be pulled from it.

Niépce's associate, Louis-Jacque-Mandé Daguerre, improved the process in 1837 by inventing the daguerreotype, which fixed an image on a silvered copper plate. This invention became a worldwide sensation. Daguerre could make duplicate copies because William Henry Fox-Talbot in 1834 had invented the negative-positive method of photographic printing with the negative image on sensitized paper. In 1840, he discovered that chemical treatments could develop and fix images from fading. By 1850, New York City had 77 daguerreotype studios, of which Mathew B. Brady's was the most celebrated. Brady would later become famous for photographing the US Civil War.

In 1861, the first colour photograph was made by the Scottish physicist James Clerk Maxwell using different coloured filters. The images were photographed by Thomas Sutton, an English inventor, who had developed the single-lens reflex plate camera in the late 1850s. In 1859, Sutton invented the panoramic camera with a wide-angle lens.

THE BICYCLE

The first two-wheeled bicycle was constructed in Germany by Baron Karl von Drais de Sauerbrun. He rode it in 1817 for 14km (9 miles) in Mannheim and exhibited it the following year in Paris before thousands of spectators. He named this prototype *draisienne* and called it a *laufmaschine* ('running machine'). It had a wooden frame and a triangle steering column with a small pole to control direction. The front wheel pivoted, and the rider had an armrest over it and a padded seat. Unfortunately, the rider had to push his feet on the ground to go forward, travelling up to 9.6km (6 miles) an hour.

The next year, the English coachmaker Denis Johnson patented a virtual copy, although he replaced the wood with metal. Called the 'dandy horse' or 'hobbyhorse', it could reach up to 16km (10 miles) an

THE MOTORCYCLE

THREE STEAM-POWERED bicycles were produced from 1867 to 1884, but the first true motorcycle, with an internal combustion petrol engine, was built in 1885 in Stuttgart, Germany, by Gottlieb Daimler and his employee, Wilhelm Maybach.

Their wooden *Reitwagen* ('riding car') had a belt drive and an upright single-cylinder engine called a grandfather clock engine. Its ignition was by a platinum tube to the combustion chamber heated by an open flame. Two outrigger wheels were added to keep it upright.

Daimler's 17-year-old son, Paul, first rode the Reitwagen for 12km (7.5 miles) – a success, although the seat caught fire from the ignition's heated tube.

Below: Daimler's *Reitwagen*, also called an *Einspur* ('single track'), led to him being dubbed 'the father of the motorcycle'.

hour. Two French brothers, Ernest and Pierre Michaux, refined this model by adding cranks and pedals at the front. Called a velocipede, it had iron rims on the wooden wheels that caused the handlebars to shake on cobblestone streets, giving it the nickname of the 'boneshaker'.

It was not until 1839 that Kirkpatrick Macmillan, the son of a Scottish blacksmith, created the look of today's bicycle by adding pedals whose movement was transmitted to cranks on the rear wheel to create a fast pace. He never patented the design and many others copied it, most notably another Scotsman, Gavin Dalzell in 1846. For nearly 50 years, Dalzell was wrongly regarded as the inventor of the bicycle.

GERMAN SCIENTISTS CARL FRIEDRICH GAUSS AND WILHELM WEBER DEVISED THE FIRST COMMERCIAL TELEGRAPH IN 1833.

The high-wheeled penny-farthing appeared in the 1870s, invented by Eugène Meyer in Paris and greatly refined by James Starley of Coventry, England. The name came from the difference in sizes between the huge front wheel and the miniature back one, like the different sizes of a penny and farthing. Its striking design made it challenging to ride, but eventually the iron wheels were replaced with hard rubber ones. Lightweight wire spokes contributed to its fast speed, leading to the sport of cycle racing. In 1885, John Kemp Starley, the nephew of James Starley, designed the Rover Safety Bicycle, which was easier to use, less dangerous and faster. More comfort was added in 1888 when Scotsman John Boyd Dunlop invented the pneumatic rubber tyre.

THE TELEGRAPH

Electricity and magnetism were considered to be separate forces until the nineteenth century, when it was discovered that both were one aspect of the same phenomenon, electromagnetism. Efforts began in America and Europe to develop an electric telegraph; the first success went to the American inventor Samuel Morse, who in 1832 submitted his idea for a patent. German scientists Carl Friedrich Gauss and Wilhelm Weber devised the first commercial telegraph in 1833 to communicate with

languished. In England in 1837, inventors William Cooke and Charles Wheatstone connected two train stations on the Great Western Railway with 21km (13 miles) of telegraph wire.

By 1838, Morse had invented his own single-wire telegraph line and, with a friend, Alfred Vail, created the system of dots and dashes that became known as Morse code. Morse tried unsuccessfully to set up a telegraph line in Europe but in 1843 won approval and funding from the US Congress to build a line from Washington, DC, to Baltimore, Maryland. Its length of 60km (35 miles) ran along a railway line with wires attached to glass insulators on poles. Construction was completed in 1844. On 24 May, Morse sent the first short message, 'What hath God wrought'.

Other inventors made legal claims that they had had the idea first, but Morse won an 1854 US Supreme Court decision giving him the patent rights. The first transatlantic telegraph cable was laid in 1858. Three years later, the American Civil War began; both sides, especially the Union, relied on telegraph communications between their forces.

Opposite: Civil War armies had to work fast between battles to erect poles and connect the ends of telegraph wire.

THE GRAPEVINE

BESIDES THE PROPERLY STRUNG telegraph lines, many lines were laid haphazardly against trees or twisted and gnarled on THE GROUND; these became known as grapevine telegraphs.

The term was first used in the 1850s among slaves and free Blacks who were forwarded news from telegraph reports about the abolition campaign and plans for war. Some reports sounded doubtful and led to the expression, 'I heard it on the grapevine', indicating an informal way of receiving news. This term was eventually applied to gossip.

Civil War armies used the telegraph on the battlefield, where the cables had to be quickly scattered about and were often tapped or cut by the enemy. About 24,150km (15,000 miles) of military telegraph cables were laid during the war, with messages sent and received in special wagons. Soldiers also called this the 'grapevine', and used the description for informal news too.

THE MACHINE GUN

The forerunner of the modern machine gun was invented by Richard Jordan Gatling in 1862 during the American Civil War. His Gatling gun was a multi-barrel machine gun operated by a crank. He had already invented a hemp-breaking machine and a steam plough when the outbreak of war turned his efforts towards the idea of a sustained rapid-firing weapon. He realized this was possible because of the army's recent shift from paper cartridges, which each had to have a separate percussion cap,

Below: A patent drawing in 1865 for Gatling's 'battery gun', a six-barrelled machine gun adopted by the US Army.

to the new brass cartridge, which had a self-contained percussion cap. In 1861, Gatling settled in Indianapolis, Indiana, and began production at the Gatling Gun Company.

Gatling's weapon had ten barrels around a central shaft. They were loaded from a cartridge container above the gun and fired when the hand crank caused a half rotation; the remaining half rotation ejected the spent cases. The .577-calibre gun could fire 350 shots a minute with an effective range of 1829m (2000yd).

Gatling gave several demonstrations to Union officers. The guns, which were moved on wheels, sold for $1000 each, and the army used 12 during the siege of Petersburg, Virginia, near the end of the war. The army asked Gatling to build a version that could be used for both long-range and close engagements. The war ended as he worked on the project, but the army adopted it the following year and would use the guns against Native Americans.

In 1884, the American inventor Hiram Maxim produced the first fully automatic single-barrel machine gun while living in London. He became a British subject in 1900 and was knighted by Queen Victoria the following year. His gun was manufactured by Vickers and used extensively in World War I.

In 1900, Gatling at the age of 82 invented a machine gun operated by electricity that could fire 3000 rounds a minute, and also one driven by gas.

THE FIRST INVENTION TO HARNESS ELECTRICITY FOR LIGHTING WAS THE CARBON-ARC LAMP, CREATED IN 1858 BY THE ENGLISH PHYSICIST AND CHEMIST MICHAEL FARADAY.

THE INCANDESCENT LAMP

The first invention to harness electricity for lighting was the carbon-arc lamp, created in 1858 by the English physicist and chemist Michael Faraday. He used an electric generator powered by steam to light a carbon-arc lamp for South Foreland Lighthouse at Dover, making it the first lighthouse to use an electric light. The lamp itself, however, was seldom used, being too bright and needing too much power.

Inventors realized that the incandescent lamp was far superior. Frederick de Moleyns received the first patent for such a lamp in 1841, but the bulb would blacken and the lamp lacked a proper vacuum tube to reduce this. One arrived in 1865 with the mercury pump, and the first reliable carbon-filament bulb was developed in 1878 by the English physicist Joseph Wilson Swan. He created a light bulb using a platinum filament in an evacuated glass tube. At the same time, Thomas Edison invented his light bulb. He would triumph commercially, because he was able to

THE LONDON UNDERGROUND

ON 9 JANUARY 1863, the Metropolitan Railway opened the world's first underground railway in London, running between Bishop's Road (now Paddington) and the City of London. Tickets for the three classes cost three, four or six pence for a single trip, and the first day saw 40,000 passengers. They referred to the carriages as 'padded cells', and the first accidents occurred a couple of months later. The steam locomotives led to the carriages and stations filling with black smoke.

In 1868, another line (now the District Line) opened between Westminster and

create a total vacuum whereas Swan could manage only a partial one. Swan developed a cellulose filament in 1881, while Edison used electroplated bamboo filaments.

After a legal dispute about patents, the two inventors formed a joint company in 1883. Edison established the Edison General Electric Company in 1890 and, after a merger in 1892 with his main competitor, the Thomson-Houston Company, the larger business

South Kensington, and the next year the first steam trains began running through the Thames Tunnel built by Isambard Kingdom Brunel and his father. In 1884, after 21 years of construction, the Inner Circle (now Circle) line opened to connect with the Metropolitan and District lines, running more than 800 trains every day. The *Times* described its trips as 'a form of mild torture'.

In 1890, the City and South London Railway opened the first deep-level railway, 18m (60ft) below the streets and running from the City of London under the Thames to Stockwell. It used electric trains to solve the problem of black smoke and eliminated the screaming whistles of the steam trains, but passengers still complained about the three carriages having no windows and the slow speed of 24km (15 miles) per hour. London's Underground system was not called the 'Tube' until the early 1900s.

The next Underground systems opened in Budapest in May 1896, Glasgow in December that year, and Boston in September 1897, where some 100,000 passengers rode the three-and-a-half-minute trip on the first day.

Left: Dignitaries took a ride on the Metropolitan Railway's first train, including future Prime Minister William Gladstone and his wife.

became the General Electric Company that still exists today.

The first city to use electric arc lamps as street lights was Paris, in 1878, followed the next year by Newcastle-upon-Tyne in the UK. The first American city to use Edison's incandescent bulbs was Cleveland, Ohio, to light a square in 1879; the first to light streets was Wabash, Indiana, the next year. London also installed this type of street light in Brixton in 1880.

ANTISEPTICS

Operations in the nineteenth century were dirty affairs conducted in unclean rooms. Surgeons failed to wash their hands, operated wearing filthy aprons, and only cleaned their instruments after use, leading to a high death rate from infection.

The British surgeon Joseph Lister based his work on the French chemist Louis Pasteur, who had proved that germs, invisible to the naked eye, were the cause of infections and disease. Lister was able to break that connection by spraying the antiseptic carbolic acid on surgical wounds and instruments, and in 1867 reported that the mortality rate on his wards had dropped.

LISTER'S METHOD WAS TO PACK AND COVER WOUNDS WITH LINT AND GAUZE SOAKED IN CARBOLIC ACID, THEN ADDING A LAYER OF TIN AND PLASTER.

One of Lister's impressive successes was with Queen Victoria. She was suffering from a large abscess under her armpit and sought help from Lister, who lived close to her Scottish residence. Before operating, Lister brought in the 'donkey engine' he had invented and had his assistant sterilize all of the operating area by spraying it with carbolic acid. Some of it unfortunately went in the queen's face. The operation may have saved her life, and Victoria's willingness to undergo Lister's spraying procedure was a firm endorsement for antiseptics.

JOSEPH LISTER

BORN A QUAKER IN Essex, England, in 1827, Joseph Lister was a son of a Fellow of the Royal Society who had built the first achromatic lens. Lister studied at the University College of the University of London and in 1852 became a fellow of the Royal College of Surgeons. He went to Edinburgh in 1853 to study under the renowned surgeon James Syme, and married Syme's daughter, Agnes. Lister was appointed a surgeon at the Edinburgh Royal Infirmary in 1856 and at Glasgow University in 1861.

Lister was later criticized for not giving credit to other members of his team in Glasgow. He had made the discoveries about antiseptics, however, and is considered the father of modern surgery.

Lister's method was to pack and cover wounds with lint and gauze soaked in carbolic acid, then adding a layer of tin and plaster. Scepticism and opposition continued among some physicians, since they were unable to see germs through their microscopes. Nevertheless, Lister's method reduced deaths and was quickly adopted in Germany, followed by the United States, France and Britain.

THE TELEPHONE

The telephone was invented by the Scottish-born American inventor Alexander Graham Bell after attempting to send several messages over a single wire, including musical tones over what he called a harmonic telegraph. When he heard his assistant, Thomas Watson, pluck a spring to reactivate a telegraph transmitter, Bell became convinced that a voice could travel over the wire. In 1876, he sent a simple current along one and quickly patented the accomplishment. On 12 March that year, he was successful in transmitting speech. Using his device, which he first called the 'electric speech machine', Bell sat in one room of a Boston boarding house and spoke to his assistant in another room, saying 'Mr Watson! Come here! I want to see you!' Watson appeared gasping, 'I heard you! I heard you!'

Below: On 18 October 1892, Bell inaugurated the 1520km (944 mile) telephone link between New York and Chicago.

ALEXANDER GRAHAM BELL

THE INVENTOR OF THE telephone was born in Edinburgh, Scotland, the son of a phoneticist and a deaf mother. The family emigrated to Canada in 1870, and the next year Bell moved to the United States to teach deaf-mute children. His idea of 'electronic speech' led him to invent the microphone. In 1872, he established a school in Boston to train teachers of the deaf. It became part of Boston University in 1873, with Bell as professor of vocal physiology. In 1877 he married one of his deaf students, Mabel Hubbard, and they would have four children.

In 1880, Bell developed more techniques for teaching the deaf. Among those he worked with was the blind and deaf woman Helen Keller. He also continued inventing, doing early work on a metal detector, creating a wireless telephone he called a 'photophone', and developing an electrical bullet probe for surgical use. In 1885, he moved to Nova Scotia, Canada, and began experiments in aviation technology. His final invention, when 75, was a fast hydrofoil. He was a founder of the National Geographic Society in 1888 and served as its president from 1896 to 1904.

Left: Helen Keller (left) met Bell as a child, and he introduced her to Anne Sullivan, her future teacher.

On 7 March 1876, Bell received patent No. 174,465 for his 'Improvement in telegraphy'. He was immediately challenged in hundreds of legal cases claiming the invention, but Bell's patent was upheld in the US Supreme Court. He said, 'I may perhaps take credit for having blazed a trail for others who came after me', and added that credit had to go to those who had made later developments of the telephone.

In 1877, Bell became the technical adviser to the new Bell Telephone Company. He owned a third of the shares but soon sold them. That same year, the first telephone exchange opened in Connecticut. Mergers later established the American Bell Telephone Company, and in 1899 it became the American Telephone and Telegraph Company (AT&T).

THE PHONOGRAPH

Victorians needed a device to record sound; it was produced by the American inventor, Thomas Edison. He called the machine a phonograph and demonstrated it in 1877. It consisted of a rotating drum covered with a tinfoil cylinder. A vibrating stylus (needle) converted the sounds on the tinfoil into a spiralling sound line of indentions on the surface. When played back, a second needle picked up sounds from the tinfoil and these were amplified.

Below: Emile Berliner's gramophone introduced the public to the flat disc that would become the shape of modern records.

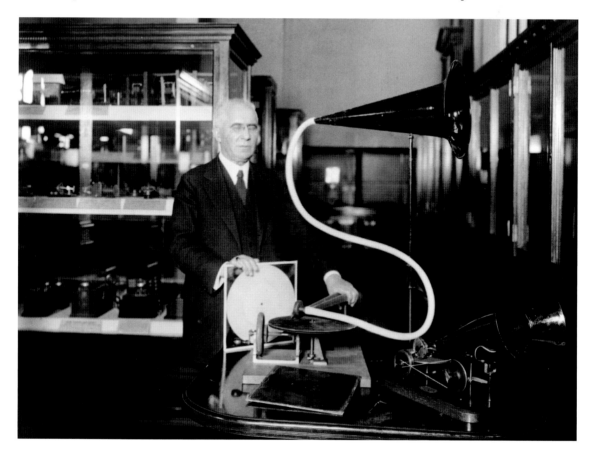

The first words that Edison recorded were 'Mary had a little lamb'. He was amazed when he heard the playback, and later said that the phonograph was his favourite invention. He suggested the device could be connected to the telephone to record conversations.

In the 1880s, Alexander Graham Bell, with others in his laboratory, made significant improvements in the phonograph. They replaced the delicate tinfoil with wax-coated cardboard cylinders that produced a higher-quality recording with a longer playing time. They also replaced the manual crank with an electric motor.

Below: Louis Pasteur successfully applied pasteurization to save France's wine and beer industries, whose products had become contaminated when exported.

In 1887, Emile Berliner, a German-born American, invented a recording machine that he named the gramophone. It had a flat horizontal disc that would be adopted for modern records. The sounds were cut into spiral sound grooves. The discs made of shellac were less fragile and unwieldy than Edison's drum, and eliminated the distortions caused by gravity. Many copies could be made from the original master disc using a mould.

Berliner was a creative inventor who also developed a transmitter to increase the weak sound of telephone transmitters, produced an acoustic tile, designed a lightweight internal-combustion motor for aircraft, and helped his son, Henry, design a helicopter that flew successfully in 1919.

VACCINATION

The French chemist Louis Pasteur's theory of germs causing disease led to his search for a vaccine – work that would establish the scientific basis for immunology. Before this, in 1862, Pasteur had already discovered that heating wine and beer to about 57°C (135°F) prevented their abnormal fermentation, leading to the widespread pasteurization process for milk.

Pasteur's first important vaccine success was inoculating chickens that had cholera. This made them resistant to the virulent strain and encouraged him to apply immunization to many other diseases. The chance for a large-scale experiment came in 1879, when an anthrax epidemic in Europe was killing sheep and infecting humans. By 1881, Pasteur had received financial support from farmers and others to conduct a large-scale public experiment on the outskirts of Paris. He selected 70 farm sheep and vaccinated half of them. After a few days, all of the vaccinated sheep had survived and the others had all died, providing Pasteur with a highly visible success.

He next turned his attention to the dreaded rabies disease. After experimenting on rabbits, in 1885 he vaccinated a 9-year-old boy, Joseph Meister, and achieved complete success. Other rabies victims around the world were soon saved by the vaccine. This would be Pasteur's finest moment, bringing him respect and fame. International funds were raised to build the Pasteur Institute in Paris, which opened in 1888.

THE FRENCH CHEMIST LOUIS PASTEUR'S THEORY OF GERMS CAUSING DISEASE LED TO HIS SEARCH FOR A VACCINE.

Below: Francis Galton opened his Anthropometric Laboratory in 1884 at London's International Health Exhibition, charging a fee to measure visitors' bodies.

FINGERPRINTING

The use of fingerprints for identity purposes was suggested in 1880 in the British scientific journal *Nature*, which described their uniqueness and permanence. The use of fingerprinting at crime scenes was proposed in 1880 by Henry Faulds, a medical missionary in Japan. Sir Francis Galton, an English scientist, first classified the arches, loops and whorls of fingerprints, and an identification system based on

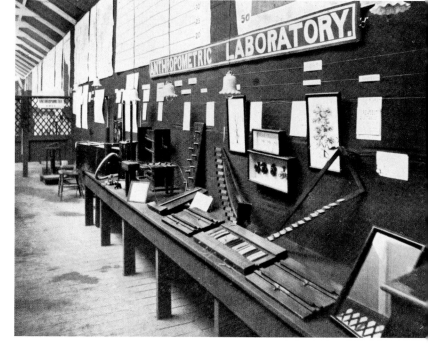

this was created in 1888 by Juan Vucetich, with the Buenos Aires police. Most Spanish-speaking nations still use Vucetich's system.

In the UK, Sir Edward Henry, later commissioner of the London Metropolitan Police, introduced the Galton-Henry fingerprint classification system to Scotland Yard in 1901. This system quickly spread in the Western world and today is the most used method for the identification of suspects. The Federal Bureau of Investigation (FBI) in the US presently has a fingerprint file of more than 250 million people.

Below: Guglielmo Marconi (left) and his assistant George Kemp receive the first wireless signals across the Atlantic in 1901.

RADIO WAVES

As important to modern life as the telegraph and telephone became, they were restricted to wires to send and receive messages, and these lines were often missing or damaged. The solution was wireless radio waves. The German scientist Heinrich Hertz in 1888 discovered electromagnetic waves, proving the theory of Scottish physicist James Clerk Maxwell that light and heat are electromagnetic radiations. Guglielmo Marconi, an Italian electrical engineer, made the first successful transmission using radio waves in 1895 over a distance of 2.5km (1.5 miles).

The following year, Marconi visited England and demonstrated his system successfully in London and

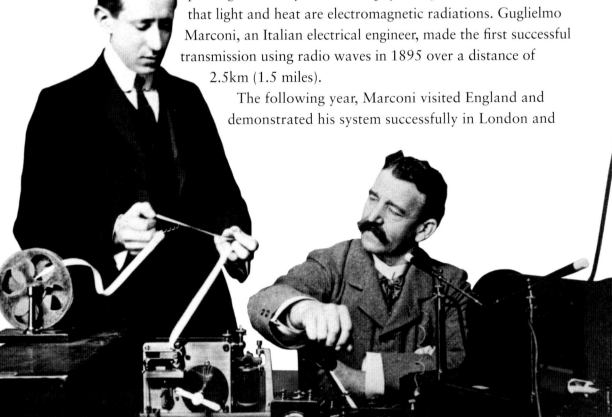

across the Bristol Channel. That year, he was awarded a patent for his 'wireless telegraphy'. In 1899, he connected England and France across the English Channel.

In 1900, Marconi received a patent for 'tuned or syntonic telegraphy', and the next year proved that his system was not affected by the Earth's curvature by sending the first wireless signals across the Atlantic, 3380km (2100 miles) from Cornwall, England, to Canada's Newfoundland. In 1902, he patented a magnetic detector that became the first wireless receiver, and in 1909 was awarded the Nobel Prize for Physics.

Messages were soon being sent to ships that could not be reached by telegraph or telephone. The first domestic 'wireless' radio broadcast to the public was sent in 1906 by the Canadian inventor Reginald Fessenden from Brant Rock in Massachusetts.

Above: The Home Insurance Building in Chicago weighed only one-third as much as a masonry building of the same height.

SKYSCRAPERS

The first modern skyscraper was the Home Insurance Building, built in Chicago in 1884. The American architect and engineer William Le Baron Jenney designed the 10-storey building, which was the first to use structural steel instead of masonry and the first tall building to be fireproofed inside and out. These features became standard and were incorporated into future skyscrapers. The building rose to 12 stories after an 1890 addition, but was demolished in 1931 to make way for another skyscraper. It began an entire architectural movement, the Chicago School, which created the 'commercial style' of square-shouldered buildings without adornment that became so popular in American cities.

Chicago was a perfect proving ground for builders. Its great fire of 1871 destroyed thousands of wooden buildings, and architects were eager to follow Jenney's revolutionary design. The city's buildings continued to rise higher until the Masonic Temple Building, built in 1892, reached a record 21 stories, as high as height restrictions then allowed. It was torn down in 1939 when a subway was being constructed.

The concept of building up instead of out especially appealed to architects in New York City who worked within the confines of Manhattan. Offices of the city's newspapers competed with impressive buildings: the *New York Tribune* (1875), the *New York Times* (1889), whose building gave the name to Times Square, and the *New York World* (1890). New York's most iconic structure, the 22-storey Flatiron Building, was completed in 1902. Its dramatic wedge-shape design was created by Daniel Burnham of the Chicago School. It was not the city's tallest, however, that record going to the 29-storey Park Row Building that had gone up in 1899. The United States had the world's tallest building for more than a century, until Malaysia built the Petronas Twin Towers in Kuala Lumpur in 1998.

HE WAS SURPRISED TO SEE THE TUBE EMIT INVISIBLE RAYS THAT CAUSED DIFFERENT CHEMICALS ON A SCREEN ACROSS THE ROOM TO GLOW.

X-RAYS

In 1895, the German scientist Wilhelm Röntgen, professor of physics at Wurzburg, Bavaria, was experimenting with a cathode ray tube (the future television) covered in black paper and in a completely dark room. He was surprised to see the tube emit invisible rays that caused different chemicals on a screen across the room to glow. His experiments found that the rays made solid materials, such as wood, paper and aluminium, become transparent.

Because Röntgen mistakenly believed the rays were not related to light, he named the phenomenon 'X-radiation'. He found that the rays made an impression on photographic plates, and among his first X-ray photographs were the bones in his wife's hand.

One of the first radiology departments in the world was set up in 1896 at the Glasgow Royal Infirmary in Scotland, where that year Dr John Hall-Edwards, a pioneer in medical X-rays, made one of the first X-ray diagnoses after finding a needle inside a woman's hand.

Röntgen was awarded the first ever Nobel Prize for Physics in 1901 for his discovery. X-rays made the inner body visible without surgery, rewriting medical diagnoses. They even helped develop modern physics.

MOTION PICTURES

The basic idea of creating apparent motion out of still photographs was first demonstrated by Eadweard Muybridge, a British-born photographer who emigrated to the United States and became famous in 1868 for photographing Yosemite Valley, California.

In 1872, the railroad magnate Leland Stanford hired Muybridge to prove that a trotting horse had all four legs off the ground at the same time during certain positions in its gait. Muybridge proved this was true in 1877 by positioning up to 24 cameras with a shutter having an exposure of 2/1000s of a second. He then invented a lantern, which he called a Zoopraxiscope, that projected images on a screen from photographs on a rotating glass disc moving so quickly as to create the illusion of motion. The Zoopraxiscope proved a sensational hit at the 1893 World's Columbian Exposition in Chicago. From 1884 to 1887, Muybridge repeated his motion studies using humans performing activities with and without clothes for the benefit of scientists and artists.

Intrigued by these results, Thomas Edison in 1889 organized a team that invented a Strip Kinetograph camera that took photographs on a strip of film. They then invented the Kinetoscope to show the results. The first Kinetoscope parlour opened in 1894,

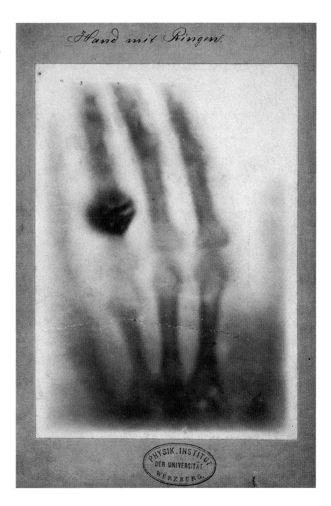

Above: Wilhelm Röntgen's first medical X-ray was of the hand of his wife, Anna Bertha, in 1895.

showing films a few seconds long for the price of five cents. In 1893, the American inventor Charles Francis Jenkins built the Phantoscope projector that could beam life-size pictures on a screen. The following year, he demonstrated it to family, friends and journalists in Richmond, Indiana. Thomas Edison bought the patent to produce his Vitascope, and on 23 April 1896 had his first commercial showing of a motion picture, at Koster and Bial's Music Hall in New York City.

Among other pioneers in motion pictures were the French brothers Auguste and Louis Lumière, who invented a single camera that both photographed and projected film at 16 frames a second. On 28 December 1895, they showed a film at the Grand Café in Paris and the next year made more than 40 motion pictures.

Below: Eadweard Muybridge's project of photographing a horse was interrupted when he was tried and acquitted of killing his wife's lover.

THOMAS EDISON

BORN IN MILAN, Ohio, Thomas Alva Edison was the seventh and youngest child of his family. He suffered from deafness and only attended a few months of school. By the age of 16, he was working as a telegrapher. In 1868, he moved to Boston, where he invented an electric vote recorder, but it failed. The following year, he went to New York and invented the Universal Stock Printer, earning $40,000 for this and other ideas.

Edison moved in 1871 to Newark, New Jersey, to work on refining the telegraph. Five years later, he settled in Menlo Park near New York City, where his first great successes were the phonograph in 1877 and the electric light bulb the next year.

Edison's wife, Mary, died in 1884, leaving him with three children. He married again two years later, and he and his second wife, Mina, settled in West Orange, New Jersey. There he worked on the phonograph again and in 1889 developed the Kinetoscope used to show motion pictures. His last project in the 1920s grew out of a request from Henry Ford and Harvey Firestone to develop artificial rubber. Edison tested thousands of plants until finding that goldenrod was a possibility. He was working on this up to his death in 1931.

CONCLUSION

The expansion in the nineteenth century of territories and ideas gave Victorians a vast canvas on which to create their vision of a modern, well-regulate life. This didn't happen easily, as the Industrial Revolution caused social upheavals and colonial wars cost countless lives. To the Victorian mind these were prices worth paying to spread their new world of morality and technology.

Progress brought riches to some, but many people struggled to avoid poverty and crime, feeling fortunate if they could simply survive. Victorians regarded social inequality at home and in colonies as the natural way of the world, content that advances in fields like transport, communications and medicine would eventually benefit all. On a personal level, people brightened their lives with a variety of amusements, from freak shows to Gothic novels, bicycles and motion pictures. Access to the mass media and entertainment would help change Victorian attitudes in the uncertain future of the twentieth century.

INDEX

PICTURE CREDITS

Alamy: 5 (Pictorial Press), 6 (Paul Fearn), 8 (HIP/Fine Art Images), 9 (Interfoto), 10 (World History Archive), 11 (Granger Collection), 12/13 (HIP/Guildhall Library & Art Gallery) 16 (Granger Collection), 17 (North Wind Picture Archive), 19 (Archive Farms, inc), 21 (Lordprice Collection), 22 (KGPA), 23 (World History Archive), 25 (Interfoto), 31 (Niday Picture Library), 32 (World History Archive), 34 (Classic Image), 36 bottom (Pictorial Press), 37 (G L Archive), 38 & 40 (World History Archive), 44 & 45 bottom (B Christopher), 45 top (Photo Researchers/ Science History Images), 46 (Hi-Story), 48 (Pictorial Press), 50 (Dinodia Photos), 54 (Photo Researchers/ Science History Images), 55 (Hi-Story), 56 (Photo Researchers/ Science History Images), 59 (World History Archive), 60 (HIP/Museum of London), 61 (World History Archive), 64 (Pictorial Press), 65 (Granger Collection), 66 (Art Collection 3), 67 (Pictorial Press), 71 (History Collections), 72 (Historical Image Collection by Bildagentur-online), 75 (AGE Fotostock/Linh Hassel), 76 (Paul Fearn), 78 (G L Archive), 79 (Classic Image), 80 (916 Collection), 86 & 88 (Lordprice Collection), 97 (Print Collector), 103 (Lordprice Collection), 113 (William Stevens), 114 (Everett Collection), 115 (Pictorial Press), 116 (Lebrecht), 118 (Niday Picture Library), 121 (Lebrecht), 122 (Art Collection 3), 123 & 124 (Pictorial Press), 133 (Granger Collection), 135 (Lebrecht), 136 (Archivart), 139 (Paul Fearn), 140 (Historical Image Archive), 143 (Peter Jordan), 147 top (B Christopher), 148 (Granger Collection), 153 (Artokoloro Quint Lox), 155 (North Wind Picture Archive), 163 (Granger Collection), 167 (Everett Collection), 170 (Lebrecht), 172 (G L Archive), 175 (Granger Collection), 176 & 178 (World History Archive), 181 (Mediscan), 182 (G L Archive), 184 (Pictorial Press), 185 (GeoPic), 186 (History Collection 2016), 187 (Everett Collection © Columbia Pictures), 188 (Ian Dagnall Computing), 192 (Pictorial Press), 195 & 198 & 199 (Granger Collection), 210 (RBM Vintage Images), 211 (Science History Images), 214 (Interfoto), 217 (Paul Fearn), 218 (Science History Images)

Alamy/Chronicle: 33, 36 top, 41, 51, 53, 57, 69, 85, 90, 95, 100, 101, 106, 111, 112, 120, 130, 131, 141, 209

Mary Evans Picture Library: 52, 62 (Elizabeth Mark Goodwin), 70, 74 (Peter Higginbotham Collection), 83, 91, 92 (National Archives, London, England), 93, 206/207 (Institute of Civil Engineers)

Getty Images: 28 (Bettmann), 49 (Photo Quest/Archive Photos), 77 (Corbis/Fine Art Photographic), 87 (Hulton), 102 (Corbis/ Stefano Bianchetti), 105 (Hulton), 108 (UIG/Leemage), 134 (Print Collector), 137 (Corbis/Photo Josse/Leemage), 173 (Hulton), 174 (The John Deakin Archive), 193 & 213 (SSPL)

Library of Congress: 14/15, 18, 24, 26, 27, 94, 98, 99, 128, 132, 144, 146, 147 bottom, 150, 152, 154, 156-159 all, 164-166 all, 177, 180, 190, 191, 197, 212, 215

Photos.com: 127, 138

Public Domain: 42, 73, 81, 109, 110, 196, 204

Shutterstock: 200 (Mmuenzi)

US Department of Defense: 160-162 all, 168, 169, 203

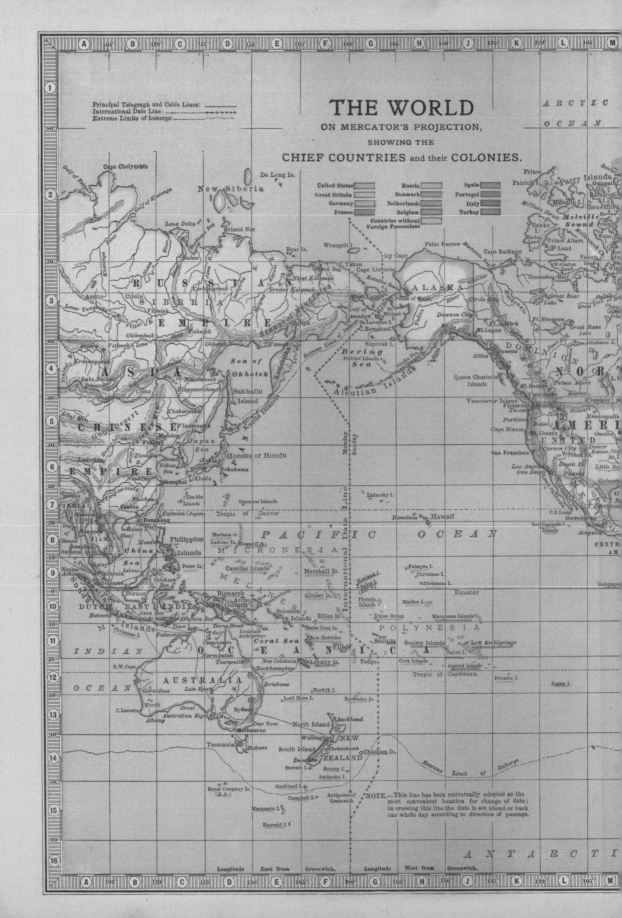

THE WORLD

ON MERCATOR'S PROJECTION,

SHOWING THE

CHIEF COUNTRIES and their COLONIES.

Principal Telegraph and Cable Lines: _____
International Date Line: ++++++
Extreme Limits of Icebergs: _____

United States	Russia	Spain
Great Britain	Denmark	Portugal
Germany	Netherlands	Italy
France	Belgium	Turkey
	Countries without Foreign Possessions	

NOTE.—This line has been universally adopted as the most convenient location for change of date; in crossing this line the date is set ahead, or back one whole day according to direction of passage.

Longitude   East from   Greenwich.   Longitude   West from   Greenwich.